Yosemite
Ultra Classics

Greg Barnes

Chris McNamara

Steve Roper

Todd Snyder

Published by
SuperTopo
2 Bradford Way
Mill Valley, CA 94941
www.supertopo.com

Topos and text by Greg Barnes, Chris McNamara, and Todd Snyder.
History by Steve Roper and Chris McNamara.
Managing Editor and Designer: Sarah Felchlin.
Editors: Sarah Felchlin and Chris McNamara.
Designers: Sarah Felchlin and David Safanda.

Front cover: Justin Bastien prepares to rappel Royal Arches.
Back cover: Todd Snyder on Lost Arrow Spire Tip.
   Photos by Corey Rich

Acknowledgements

Many thanks go to the following people who submitted feedback: Jerry Anderson, Robert Behrens, Andy Bourne, Lincoln Else, Steve Fettke, Mark Gosselin, Brad Goya, James C. Holmes, Jay Kinghorn, Mark Kroese, Michael McGuinn, Kristin Tara McNamara, Mike Nelson, Robin Weber, Jeff Rutland, Erik Sandelin, and Greg Schaffer.
   Special thanks to David Safanda and Janine Patittuci for their brilliant help with the cover design and images. Thank you to Tresa Black for the great photo of Steve Roper.

Library of Congress Cataloging-in-Publication Data

McNamara, Chris, 1978-
 Yosemite ultra classics / by Chris McNamara, Greg Barnes, and Todd
Snyder.-- 1st ed.
     p. cm.
  ISBN 0-9672391-2-5 (pbk. : alk. paper)
  1. Rock climbing--California--Yosemite Valley--Guidebooks. 2.
Yosemite Valley (Calif.)--Guidebooks. I. Barnes, Greg, 1971- II.
Snyder, Todd, 1963- III. Title.
  GV199.42C22 Y6796 2002
  796.52'23'09794447--dc21

                            2002008071

Contents

ACCESS: It's every climber's concern

The Access Fund, a national, non-profit climbers organization, works to keep climbing areas open and to conserve the climbing environment. Need help with closures? Land acquisition? Legal or land management issues? funding for trails and other projects? Starting a local climbers' group? CALL US!

Climbers can help preserve access by being committed to leaving the environment in its natural state. Here are some simple guidelines:

•**ASPIRE TO CLIMB WITHOUT LEAVING A TRACE,** especially in environmentally sensitive areas like caves. Chalk can be a significant impact on dark and porous rock—don't use it around historic rock art. Pick up litter, and leave trees and plants intact.

•**DISPOSE OF HUMAN WASTE PROPERLY** Use toilets whenever possible. If toilets are not available, dig a "cat hole" at least six inches deep and 200 feet from any water, trails, campsites, or the base of climbs. *Always pack out toilet paper.* On big wall routes, use a "poop tube" and carry waste up and off with you (the old "bag toss" is now illegal in many areas).

•**USE EXISTING TRAILS** Cutting switchbacks causes erosion. When walking off-trail, tread lightly, especially in the desert where cryptogamic soils (usually a dark crust) take thousands of years to form and are easily damaged. Be aware that "rim ecologies" (the clifftop) are often highly sensitive to disturbance.

•**BE DISCREET WITH FIXED ANCHORS** *Bolts are controversial and are not a convenience—don't place them unless they are really necessary.* Camouflage all anchors. Remove unsightly slings from rappel stations (better to use steel chain or welded cold shuts). Bolts sometimes can be used proactively to protect fragile resources—consult with your local land manager.

•**RESPECT THE RULES** and speak up when other climbers don't. Expect restrictions in designated wilderness areas, rock art sites, caves, and in sensitive wildlife areas such as nesting sites for birds of prey. *Power drills are illegal in Wilderness and all national parks.*

•**PARK AND CAMP IN DESIGNATED AREAS** Some climbing areas require a permit for overnight camping.

•**MAINTAIN A LOW PROFILE** Leave the boom box and day-glo clothing at home. The less climbers are heard and seen, the better.

•**RESPECT PRIVATE PROPERTY** Be courteous to land owners. Don't climb where you're not wanted.

•**JOIN THE ACCESS FUND** To become a member, make a tax-deductible donation of $25.

THE ACCESS FUND
*Keeping climbing areas open and
conserving the climbing environment*
P.O. Box 17010
Boulder, CO 80308

A deadly bolt more than 20 years old ... one of several
thousand on popular climbs throughout the United States.

A new bolt rated to over 5,000 pounds. The ASCA
wants to replace the bad bolt above with one of these.

Bad Bolts Kill

We need YOUR help. The American Safe Climbing Association has helped replace more
than 3,000 bolts throughout the country. We estimate that there are more than 20,000 bad
bolts remaining on popular climbs today. Your $50 donation will make at least one route
safe...and that one route could be the next one you climb. The ASCA would like to get
there before you do.

**Does your crag need
re-bolting? Please
contact us.**

asca
American Safe Climbing Association

❏ $25 Supporter   ❏ $50 Contributor   ❏ $100 Advocate   ❏ $500 Lifer

Name

Address

E-Mail/Phone

All contributors receive the ASCA newsletter.
Make checks payable to: ASCA, 2 Bradford Way, Mill Valley, CA 94941
Phone 650-843-1473 www.safeclimbing.org

The American Safe Climbing Association is a 501(c)3 organization and contributions are tax deductible.

Warning!

Climbing is an inherently dangerous sport in which severe injuries or death may occur. Relying on the information in this book may increase the danger.

When climbing you can only rely on your skill, training, experience and conditioning. **If you have any doubts as to your ability to safely climb any route in this guide, do not try it.**

    This book is neither a professional climbing instructor nor a substitute for one. **It is not an instructional book. Do not use it as one.** It contains information that is nothing more than a compilation of opinions about climbing the rock climbs in Yosemite Valley. **Those opinions are neither facts nor promises.** Treat the information as opinions and nothing more. Do not substitute these opinions for your own common sense and experience.

Assumption of Risk

There may be errors in this book resulting from the inadvertent mistakes of the authors and/or the people with whom they consulted. The information was gathered from a variety of sources, which may not have been independently verified. Those who provided the information may have made mistakes in their descriptions. The authors may have made mistakes in their conveyance of the information in this book. **They cannot, therefore, guarantee the correctness of any of the information contained in the book.** The topographical maps, the photo-diagrams, the difficulty ratings, the protection ratings, the approach and/or descending information, the suggestions about equipment and other matters may be incorrect or misleading. Fixed protection may not be where indicated, may be absent, or may be unreliable. **You must keep in mind that the information in this book may be erroneous and use your own judgement when choosing, approaching, climbing or descending from a route described in this book.**

DO NOT USE THIS BOOK UNLESS YOU ASSUME THE RISK OF ITS ERRORS OF REPORTAGE OR OF JUDGMENT AND OF ITS OTHER DEFECTS.

Disclaimer of Warranties

THE AUTHORS AND PUBLISHER WARN THAT THIS BOOK CONTAINS ONLY THE AUTHORS' OPINION ON THE SUBJECTS DISCUSSED. THEY MAKE NO OTHER WARRANTIES, EXPRESS OR IMPLIED, OF MERCHANTABILITY, FITNESS FOR PURPOSE, OR OTHERWISE, AND IN ANY EVENT, THIER LIABILITY FOR BREACH OF ANY WARRANTY OR CONTRACT WITH RESPECT TO THE CONTENT OF THIS BOOK IS LIMITED TO THE PURCHASE PRICE OF THE BOOK. THEY FURTHER LIMIT TO SUCH PURCHASE PRICE THIER LIABILITY ON ACCOUNT OF ANY KIND OF NEGLIGENT BEHAVIOR WHATSOEVER ON THIER PART WITH RESPECT TO THE CONTENTS OF THIS BOOK.

Introduction

by Chris McNamara

When Yosemite climbing legend Allen Steck was asked recently, "Are there any significant first ascents left in Yosemite?" He replied, "Only about 100,000." Yosemite is a climber's paradise with literally thousands of documented routes—a mind-blowing selection of quality rock climbing opportunities. With so many routes it is hard to figure out where to start. In our Yosemite Ultra Classics pack we've tried to give you the benefit of local knowledge, pin-pointing Yosemite's most classic routes in the 5.4 to 5.10 range.

Welcome to Yosemite Ultra Classics

Our goal in this guidebook is to provide the best beta for the best Yosemite routes. We chose these routes because of their exceptional rock quality, elegant lines, and outstanding views.

Many of these routes played an historic role in the development of Yosemite rock climbing. As we do in all of our SuperTopo guidebooks, we've taken the time to provide you with the history for each route as well as the climbing info. If you're like us you'll find your climb enhanced by the rich history and colorful characters who first pioneered the climbs.

We hope you enjoy climbing these routes as much as we do. If you need to choose what climbs to do in a limited time period, you can be assured that these routes offer a superb experience.

Essential Yosemite Beta

You will find a wealth of Yosemite information and links on the SuperTopo web site. We encourage you to check the web site as it will have more current beta than we can provide for you here. However,

we've included a summary of all you need to know in this introduction. For the latest info, visit:
www.supertopo.com/climbingareas/yosemite.html
There you will find essential beta on:
• Climbing safety
• Getting there
• When to climb
• Road conditions call: 209-372-0200
• Staying in the park
• Food
• Climbing gear and climbing guides
• Bears

About the Ultra Classics Crags

When learning any crack technique, it is best to start on toprope climbs and then move onto short pitches, then longer pitches, and finally multi-pitch climbs. The following five crags are great for mastering the essential techniques.

Swan Slab (5.1-5.10c)

Swan Slab offers Yosemite Valley's most accessible 5.1-5.7 topropes and short leads. A crowded but excellent place to get acquainted with Yosemite granite.

Knob Hill (5.7-5.10a)

This is a great step up from Swan Slab. Knob Hill offers straight-in cracks and face moves on enormous knobs. Practice longer one-pitch leads here.

Sunnyside Bench (5.7-5.10d)

Sunnyside Bench is a mandatory stop on Yosemite Valley's moderate crack climbing circuit. The area enjoys the unique ambiance of the (seasonally) booming Lower Yosemite Fall.

Church Bowl (5.4-5.11)

Located between Yosemite Village and the Ahwahnee Hotel, Church Bowl is the Valley's most accessible crag for easy and moderate routes. These routes offer great training for everything from classic Yosemite chimneys to thin piton scars (for both aid and free climbing practice) to hand jams.

El Capitan Base (5.7-5.11b)

With a 3000-foot wall above, the base of El Capitan may be the most spectacular

Yosemite. It also happens that the routes are among the best in

The Ultra Classics Climbs

Few of the Ultra Classics routes are easy (in Yosemite there are few easy routes) but most offer moderate climbing with short approaches and solid protection. Though these climbs are especially appealing to Valley newcomers, climbers of all experience and ability will enjoy them.

Munginella (5.6, 3 pitches)
This is a pleasant introduction to Yosemite granite. All three pitches are sustained and challenging for their 5.6 grade.

After Six (III 5.7, 6 pitches)
After Six is a popular introduction to Yosemite multi-pitch climbing. The Pitch 1 crux is a little tricky and polished while the rest of the pitches are sustained but more moderate. A great mixture of cracks and face moves.

Half Dome, Snake Dike (III 5.7 R, 8 pitches)
Climbing this route is an incredible experience. Snake Dike winds its way up the southeast face of Half Dome—Yosemite's most renowned feature. The dike itself is one of Yosemite's extraordinary climbing features.

Selaginella (5.8, 4 pitches)
With features ranging from lieback cracks and steep faces to offwidths and chimneys, Selaginella requires a full arsenal of climbing techniques. Prepare for committing and sustained 5.7 and 5.8 cracks all the way to the route's great final crux.

Nutcracker (III 5.8, 5 pitches)
This is a climb you will do again and again. Five pitches of varied climbing includes jams, stems, liebacks, and face climbing. Be careful on the runout crux.

Higher Cathedral Rock, Braille Book (III 5.8, 6 pitches)
The distinctly un-Yosemite juggy face holds make Braille Book a must-do. The high points are the views of the Cathedral Spires, a surprise view of a giant chasm high on the route, and the unforgettable final pitch of huge 5.4 jugs on a steep spectacular wall.

Higher Cathedral Spire, Regular Route (III 5.9, 5 pitches)
Over sixty years after the first ascent, Higher Cathedral Spire remains a challenge. Unlike most rock in Yosemite, the southwest face contains numerous face holds and fractured, loose rock. The wild and exposed moves around the "Rotten Chimney" are terrifying even with sticky rubber and cams. Imagine the first ascensionists navigating this pitch with tennis shoes and ropes made of manila.

North Dome, South Face (III 5.8, 8 pitches)
The South Face of North Dome has long been overlooked. Though not quite as classic as its neighbor, Crest Jewel, this route offers quality moves worthy of the long approach. The main course is a 300-foot 5.7 lieback arch.

Commitment (5.9, 3 pitches)
This climb warms you up with two straightforward pitches then blasts you with an intense and memorable crux. Although this is a first 5.9 Valley route for many climbers, there is nothing easy about Commitment.

Middle Cathedral Rock, Central Pillar of Frenzy (III 5.9, 5 pitches)
Rising from the heart of Middle Cathedral Rock, Central Pillar of Frenzy is one of the most popular 5.9 crack climbs in Yosemite. The route offers five pitches of excellent jamming with everything from fingers to chimneys.

Royal Arches (IV 5.10b or 5.7 A0, 16 pitches)
Royal Arches is a wandering adventure up 16 pitches of 5.7 or easier climbing, with a fun pendulum that can be freed at 5.10b. This route is the easiest way to climb 1,400 feet in Yosemite.

Middle Cathedral Rock, East Buttress (IV 5.10c or 5.9 A0, 11 pitches)
Pitch after pitch of moderate Yosemite cracks are occasionally interrupted with short, well-protected crux sections. The view of El Capitan is astounding and only surpassed by the dreamy climbing moves.

Lost Arrow Spire Tip (III 5.7 C2, 2 pitches)
Lost Arrow Spire is Yosemite's most striking pinnacle. The appeal lies in its fantastic form as well as the unique rope trick, a tyrolean traverse, required to escape the summit. Though reaching the tip requires only 250 feet of climbing, 1,500 feet of exposure gives this climb a distinct big wall feeling.

Half Dome, Regular Northwest Face (VI 5.12 or 5.8 C1, 23 pitches)
Because of the long approach and north-facing orientation, the Regular Route has an alpine quality not found on other popular Yosemite walls. The climbing starts off wandering at a low angle and gradually grows steeper and gets better. The last seven pitches are spectacular.

Crack Climbing 101

Crack climbing is much harder to learn than face climbing. While grabbing an edge is intuitive, there is nothing intuitive about jamming your hands and feet into a crack. The experience is awkward at first and will probably result in pain, swelling, and blood loss.

So why bother thrashing yourself up cracks? Because like all things worthy, a rough learning period leads to extensive rewards. It is because crack climbing is challenging that it is so fulfilling. It is hard to find a face climb that gives you the same bliss as floating your way up a perfect Yosemite crack.

My first crack experience was the standard tale of terror and humility. On a one-day ascent of The Nose, I took the lead above Sickle Ledge confident I would cruise up the Stoveleg Cracks. Even though I was comfortable sport climbing 5.11 and had done laps on the 5.10 gym cracks, I barely made it through one 5.9 lead before both my head and forearms were mush. The exposure, the endurance, and the subtle technique were all too much. I handed the rack to my partner and jumared to the top.

It was only after a determined and patient apprenticeship that I learned to climb Yosemite cracks. What did I do? I followed a series of progressively more

David Safanda

difficult climbs—most of which are offered in this SuperTopo guide. First, I went to crags such as Sunnyside Bench and El Capitan Base to work out the techniques. Then I applied those techniques to progressively harder multi-pitch routes including Munginella, Nutcracker, and the East Buttress of Middle Cathedral. It wasn't long before my relationship with Yosemite cracks turned from aversion to addiction.

Even if you are a proficient face climber, your first crack climbs will feel awkward for two reasons. First, while the motion of grabbing a face hold comes naturally to most of us, the technique of jamming a hand or foot in a crack could not feel more awkward. A hand jam requires a complex and subtle sensitivity to the inside of a crack. You need to know exactly where to place your hand and how hard to jam it. Unlike a crimp where you monitor the pressure just in your fingertips, on a jam you are usually making subtle adjustments with your entire hand. The process of jamming is hard to describe and generally the only way to learn it is through attacking the cracks with determination and patience.

The second reason that crack climbing feels so hard is that it requires awkward coordination of all the limbs. On a face climb, you usually have many options for hand and foot placement to keep your body in balance. On a Yosemite crack climb, there are not many options for footholds and handholds—you are usually jamming them in the crack. This means that balance and body positioning become much more important.

Unlike sandstone or basalt cracks, the granite cracks of Yosemite vary in size frequently. A route can start as tips lieback, turn into an offwidth, and finish with hand jams. Every climb in Yosemite requires a variety of skills and any weakness you have in a particular technique will be made readily apparent.

The techniques below are listed from thinnest to widest starting with lieback and finger cracks and moving all the way to chimneys. While *Yosemite Ultra Classics* offers a good introduction to crack techniques, to become a crack master you will need to read all the technique books you can get your hands on, consult a professional guide, and pick the brains of as many talented climbers as you can.

Lieback Cracks

Liebacking offers the easiest transition from face climbing to crack climbing. In fact, many first-time crack climbers will try to lieback cracks that are most efficiently climbed with straight-in jamming techniques. While liebacking is fun and often necessary, it is important to only use the lieback technique when there is no other way to jam a crack. Why avoid a technique that seems more intuitive and less painful than jamming a crack? While liebacking may feel natural, it is the most strenuous way to climb a crack. You must constantly apply tension to the entire body, especially the arms, which quickly drains the whole body. In addition, it is difficult to place protection. When you lieback it is often impossible to see your placements. There is nothing scarier than liebacking fifteen feet above your last piece only to realize you are too pumped to let go with one hand and place a piece.

So when should you lieback? Here are

some examples. On **Oaktree Flake (5.5)**, the crack is too wide and awkward to jam. On **La Cosita, Right (5.9)**, the crack is an off size for finger jams so a short lieback sprint is necessary. On the **South Face of North Dome (5.8)**, Pitches 5-7 ascend a long 2-3" crack that is too awkward to jam straight in and must be liebacked. A great first lieback lead is the sustained and well-protected **Church Bowl Lieback (5.8)**. For more difficult moves, try out **Lemon (5.9)** at Sunnyside Bench. This is a scary lead, but a great toprope.

Finger Cracks

After lieback cracks, finger cracks provide the next easiest transition from face climbing to crack climbing. Unlike lieback cracks, finger cracks require jamming: the technique of torquing your fingers in the crack with just the right pressure. With finger cracks (and all cracks for that matter) the trick is to jam your fingers and toes with just enough pressure to stay in, but not so much pressure that you draw blood and waste energy. This is no easy task.

Pine Line (5.7) is a great introduction to finger crack technique. On this climb you will negotiate pods and insecure finger locks. **Grant's Crack (5.9)** is the most accessible 5.9 finger crack in Yosemite. Just to the left of Pine Line is the first pitch of the **Salathé Wall (5.10c)**, an exquisite finger crack. This pitch requires careful balance between powerful finger locks and delicate stems. Another great 5.10 is **Revival (5.10a)**, which can be easily toproped after climbing **Church Bowl Lieback (5.8)**. **Lazy Bum (5.10d)**, located at Sunnyside Bench, is another technical finger crack that is easy to toprope.

Hand Cracks

Euphoria is climbing a Yosemite hand crack. Your hands set securely in crack, toes comfortably jammed below, one slammer jam after another—this is truly the image of the perfect climb. On finger cracks your hands are usually secure while your feet are tenuously jammed or smeared. On fist and offwidth cracks your feet are usually secure while your arms are awkwardly cammed. On the delightful hand cracks, however, both your hands and feet are securely and snugly wedged in the crack.

The most popular climb to start out with is the first pitch of the polished and challenging **Jamcrack (5.7)**. Two other accessible and classic hand cracks are **Pot Belly (5.7)** and **Penelope's Problem (5.7)**. Once solid in the 5.7 realm, check out the sustained and wild **Ejesta (5.8)** at Reed's Pinnacle Area. This uncrowded classic features a laser-cut hand and fist crack on the second pitch. **Bishop's Terrace (5.8)** is perhaps the best hand crack of its grade in the Valley and is a must-do. For a big step up in difficulty, check out **Reed's Pinnacle Direct (5.10a)**. The steep and unrelenting hand and fist jams will test your ability to stay relaxed and place gear strategically so as not to run out!

Further into 5.10 country is **Moby Dick, Center (5.10a)** located at the base of El Capitan. You start with finger locks and the crack gradually widens from hands to fist to offwidth, all of which is easy to protect. The next step up in difficulty is **Sacherer Cracker (5.10a)**, one of the best 5.10 pitches in Yosemite. 150 feet up you will be shocked with a dramatic offwidth finish.

Fist and Offwidth Cracks and Chimneys

Now we will enter the domain of the dreaded Yosemite wide cracks. If there is one thing that first time Yosemite visitors fear it is a steep and polished fist crack, offwidth, or chimney. While in many climbing areas you can avoid wide cracks, in Yosemite it is rare for a multi-pitch climb not to have at least a few sections of mandatory wide crack moves. It is here that the refined art of "thrashing" comes into play.

The best moderate fist cracks are at Knob Hill. **Turkey Pie (5.7)** delivers sustained moves while **Anti-Ego Crack (5.7)** involves just a short section of fist jams (which you can lieback around).

A great first offwidth lead is **Center Route (Pitch 1, 5.7)** at Reed's Pinnacle Area. This climb has tons of 5.4-5.6 chimney and offwidth moves, much of which can be protected with large cams. Another great offwidth climb in the Reed's Pinnacle area

is **Bombs Away Left (5.8)**. The protection opportunities are relatively abundant for an offwidth climb. Church Bowl is the best spot in Yosemite to learn chimney technique. The following circuit of three climbs will hone this challenging skill. Start on **Aunt Fanny's Pantry (5.4)**. Though not particularly aesthetic, this is a great first chimney lead. For a step up in difficulty, move left to **Uncle Fanny (5.7)**, a great chimney that is well-protected with medium cams. Finally, move over to the intimidating **Church Bowl Chimney (5.6)**.

Once you have climbed a bunch of 5.6-5.9 one-pitch offwidths and chimneys, you will be ready for some of the most classic multi-pitch climbs in Yosemite. **Braille Book (5.8)** is an exceptional climb with a few sections of airy 5.8 offwidth that must be stemmed around.

Getting There

Air Travel

You have many airport options. The closest major international airports to Yosemite are either Oakland International or San Francisco International. The Oakland airport is preferable as it is less chaotic, easier to navigate, and closer to the Valley. Sacramento International is even easier to navigate, but connects to less airports. Fresno Yosemite International Airport is still closer to Yosemite, but offers the fewest flights. Some climbers who are planning extended trips in the United States fly into Los Angeles International Airport which is about seven hours from Yosemite.

Bus Travel

From any airport, you will need to either drive or take a bus to Yosemite. Greyhound Bus offers trips throughout the United States at reasonable rates. To get to Yosemite from the west side of the Sierra Nevada, you will need to take a Greyhound Bus to Merced, CA and then take the Via Bus for the final leg in Yosemite Valley. During the summer only, you can reach Yosemite from the east side of the Sierra Nevada by the YARTS bus.

Car Travel

Many people stay in Yosemite without a car. Renting a car is expensive and it is possible to reach most climbing areas in Yosemite by a free shuttle bus. The shuttle does not serve areas west of Camp 4, including El Capitan, Leaning Tower, Cookie Cliff, and Arch Rock. To reach these areas without a car you will need to hitchhike or ride a bike.

If you do want a car, you can rent one at any airport or major city. International climbers who stay in the United States for more than a month often buy a cheap used car in San Francisco or Los Angeles and sell it (or scrap it) at the end of their trip.

When to Climb

Yosemite has some of the best weather of any climbing area on earth. That said, it could storm at any time in Yosemite, and often heavily. Climbers should always prepare for the worst on a multi-day climb by bringing adequate bivy gear. The best times to climb are in the spring and fall. The summer can also be great once you get a few pitches up and out of the heat. In the winter, the Valley empties of both tourists and climbers, giving a much more pristine feel to the climbs. Winter can have good climbing weather but can also have months of uniquely wet and severe Sierra storms. Road info and weather reports can be found on the Internet or by calling 209-372-0200.

Seasons

Nov. 15–March The walls and Valley are relatively empty with usually at least one five-day spell of good weather per month. During a mild winter one to two weeks of great weather per month are common. On any winter ascent prepare for the absolute worst, as Pacific storms can last up to a week or longer and bring heavy snow and rain.

April–May 15 Walls and the Valley are still uncrowded, but there is a 50/50 chance of getting either good or miserable weather. This is also the time of some of the wettest Pacific storms.

May 15–June Perfect weather and big crowds both in the Valley and on the walls.

July–Aug The Valley is still crowed with tourists, but the climbs are uncrowded. While valley floor temperatures are often in the 90s and 100s, temperatures on the walls 500 feet above the Valley or higher are usually comfortable in the 70s and low 80s. Be prepared with plenty of extra water and if things really heat up, consider heading up to Tuolumne.

Sept.–Nov. 15 The Valley is crowded with tourists and walls are crowded. Mostly cooler weather with an occasional heat wave. The first winter storm usually arrives in late October or early November.

Staying in the Park

Yosemite Valley is a small city. The bad news is that the many buildings, restaurants, stores, and motel-like rooms take away from the natural beauty of the park. The good news is that these same things make Valley living convenient. You will find restaurants, groceries, climbing gear, a medical clinic, motels, swimming pools, rafts, bike rentals, and, if you find yourself in an unfortunate situation, a jail.

Camping

Camp 4 is the historical center of American climbing. It is also the only walk-in campground and the cheapest place to stay. No reservations are required but during peak season (May–October) expect a long wait to secure a campsite. The cost is $5 per person per night with a 14-day limit on your stay. Info on Yosemite campgrounds is now available online. Here is a great site to check the campground availability. Call 800-436-PARK to make reservations for other campsites or make reservations online.

There are a variety of places to camp outside the park boundary. Check out the Forest Service web site for more info.

Lodges and Cabins

In addition to campsites, there are also more plush accommodations available in Yosemite. If you are ready to pay the big bucks, you can stay at the lovely Ahwahnee Hotel, or for a more modest price you can crash in a motel-like room at Yosemite Lodge or a canvas topped cabin in Curry

Village. Also, a selection of vacation homes are located just minutes out of the Valley in Foresta (with views of the summit of El Capitan and Half Dome!). In the summertime, your best bet is to make reservations well in advance of your visit. Spaces fill up early for lodges and cabins in the tourist season of June to September.

Food

Groceries are available in the Valley at the Village Store, Curry Village Store, or Lodge Store. It is much cheaper to buy groceries in Oakdale, Merced, or Oakhurst on the drive to Yosemite.

There are a variety of restaurants in the Valley that serve everything from pizza and deli sandwiches to the spendy stuff at the Ahwahnee Hotel. Here is a quick listing of some of the Valley restaurants by location:
Yosemite Lodge: "The Caff" (cafeteria), Garden Terrace (all-you-can-eat), Broiler Room (moderate prices, good food), Mountain Room Bar.
Yosemite Village: Degnan's Deli, pizza, Pasta Place, burger stand.
Curry Village: Pizza Deck (with bar), cafeteria, burger stand.

Showers and Laundry

Showers cost $2 (towel included) and are available at Housekeeping or Curry Village. Laundry is available at housekeeping.

Climbing Gear and Climbing Guides

The Mountain Shop (209-372-8396), located in Curry Village, offers a selection of portaledges, haulbags, and just about every piece of gear you will need. You can get climbing instruction, arrange for a guide, and also rent gear from the Yosemite Mountaineering School and Guide Service. There are a variety of climbing shops in the San Francisco Bay Area where you can purchase gear. In San Francisco: Mission Cliffs and The North Face. In Berkeley: REI, Wilderness Exchange, Berkeley Ironworks, and Marmot Mountain Works.

If you are coming from the east side of the Sierra, then visit Wilson's Eastside Sports or Mammoth Mountaineering Supply, which both have an extensive selection of rock climbing and mountaineering gear.

Bears

In 2001, property damage caused by bears exceeded $30,000. Bears have damaged cars for as little as a stick of gum or an empty soda can. If you want what's yours to remain yours, remember three things: bears are hungry, smart, and strong.

When bears smell food, even if it's locked in your trunk or glove compartment, they shift into high gear. They get turned on by odors of containers that used to contain food. They even go for toothpaste and sunscreen. Bears don't need to smell food; they see something like a grocery bag or an ice chest, and associate it with food. In fact, they don't even need to see that much. If a bear sees clutter inside a car, he'll think, "I wonder what's under all that stuff?" and go to work.

Breaking into a car is a trivial exercise for a bear. He inserts his claws at the top of the door frame and pulls down. Then he climbs in and trashes the car. You can't outsmart or out-muscle a bear. Unless you are on a wall (and bears have been known to poach there, too), stash your food in one of the bear-proof storage lockers provided by the Park Service. For more info check out the Park Service's bear page and weekly bear bulletin.

Rest Days

What do you do when Valley temperatures hit the 90s? Head for the water. Rent rafts from Curry Village and float down the Merced River or dip into the water at El Capitan Meadow. If you are willing to drive 40 minutes, there are two great swimming holes outside of the Park boundaries. About 10 miles west of the Highway 120 entrance station, take a left immediately after a large bridge. Here you will have your choice of jumping off 15- to 25-foot cliffs or just kicking back next to the water. About 15 miles west of the Highway 140 entrance station is the Octagon, which features a rope swing, sketchy cliff and tree jumps, and great spots to kick back and have a BBQ. The directions to this place are more devious so you will have to hunt down a local Yosemite climber for info.

Ref Size*	BD Camalots	CCH Aliens	Metolius Cams	Trango Big Bros	Wild Country Friends
0.4"	.1 red	.33 black	00 gray		
0.5"	.2 yellow	.375 blue	0 purple		0 red
0.6"	.3 purple	.5 green	1 blue		.5 orange
0.75"	.4 gray	.75 yellow	2 yellow		1 yellow
1"	.5 pink	1 red	3 orange		1.25 brown
1.25"	.75 green	1.5 orange	4 red		1.5 sky
1.5"	1 red	2 purple	5 black		2 pink
1.75"	1 red	2.5 gray	6 green		2.5 royal
2"	2 yellow	2.5 gray	7 blue		3 navy
2.5"	2 yellow		8 purple		3.5 purple
3"	3 blue		9 burgundy		4 black
3.5"	3.5 gray		10 dark blue		4 black
3.5-4.5"	4 purple			1 red	5 silver
4.5-5.5"	4.5 red			2	
5.5-7"	5 green			3 green	6 plum
7-8"				3 green	
8-12"				4 blue	

* "Ref size" is the optimal crack width for a given camming unit. It is not the range given by the manufacturer.

Topo Symbols

Right-facing corner		Roof	⊥⊥⊥⊥	Bolt	x
Left-facing corner		Ledge	⊤⊤⊤⊤	Rappel anchor	
		Slab	///		
Straight-in crack		Belay station	❶	Face climbing	
Groove		Pitch length	130'●	Pine Tree	
Arete				Oak-like Tree	
Flake		Optional belay	○	Bush	
				Knob	o
Chimney		False belay	⊘	Hole	●

Notes on Rack

– "nuts" refers to any nut, stopper, or chock. "micro"= #1,2; "sml"= #3-5; "med"= #6-8; "lrg"= #9-13
– for cams, "2 ea .75-1.5" means bring two sets of all sizes between .75" and 1.5". Check the cam size chart to see which cam corresponds to which crack size.

Notes on Topo

– "belay takes .6-1" means, while leading the pitch, save enough .6-1" cams and nuts to build a natural anchor.
– a number next to a tree is its height.

Topo abbreviations

ow = offwidth
lb = lieback
p = fixed piton
R = runout (dangerous fall)

Metric system conversions

1 inch = 2.54 centimeters
1 foot = 0.35 meters
100 feet = 30.5 meter
50 yards = 45.7 meters ˙

Overview graphics

Low-clearance dirt road	● ● ● ● ● ● ● ● ●
High-clearance dirt road	
Road or State Route	——(10)——
Federal Highway	▬▬(10)▬▬
Park service trail	– – – – – – –
Climbers' trail	··············
Cross-country trail	· · · · · · · · · ·

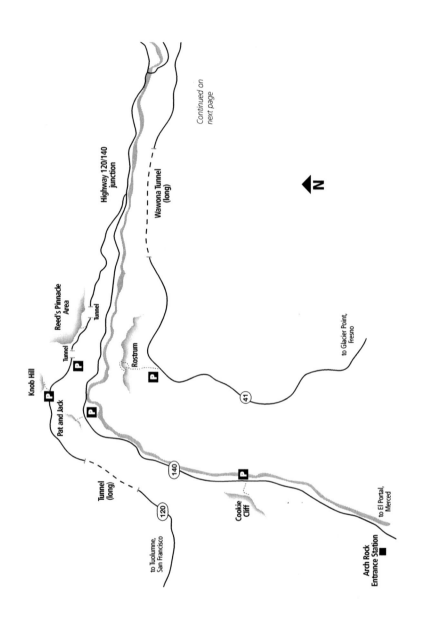

Continued on next page

N

Highway 120/140 junction

Wawona Tunnel (long)

Reed's Pinnacle Area

Tunnel

Tunnel

Rostrum

Knob Hill

Tunnel

Pat and Jack

to Glacier Point, Fresno

41

140

Tunnel (long)

120

to Tuolumne, San Francisco

Cookie Cliff

Arch Rock Entrance Station

to El Portal, Merced

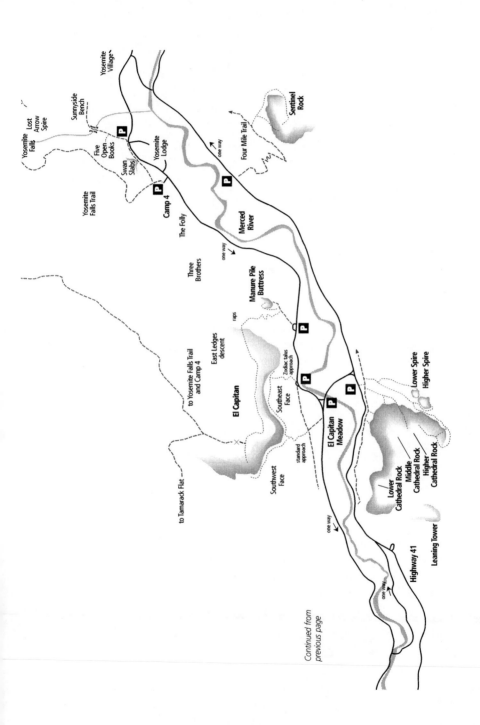

Continued from previous page

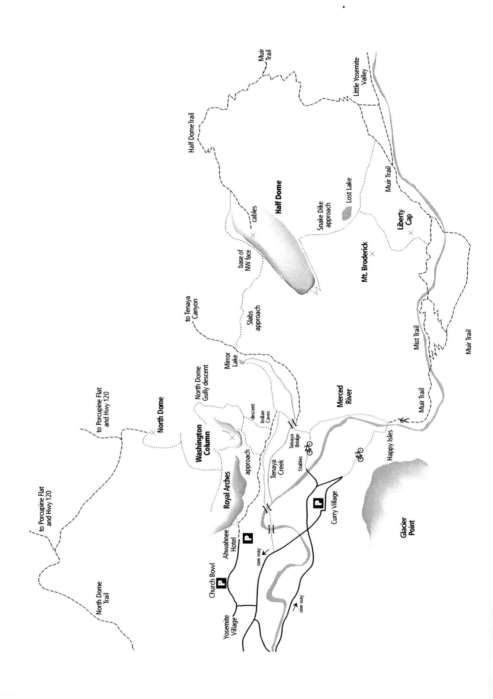

Get the color eBook of Yosemite Ultra Classics

Yosemite Ultra Classics

Greg Barnes
Chris McNamara
Todd Snyder

A color version of this guidebook is available for only $9.95 at the SuperTopo web site. The guidebook is in Adobe PDF format and formatted for easy printing on your inkjet printer. Our online guides offer many cool features not available in traditional print guidebooks:
- print out only the pages you want for each climb (no more tearing pages out of your guidebook or carrying the book up a climb)
- get all the topos and photos in full color
- frequent updates mean you know you have the most current and accurate information

For more information and a free sample, visit www.supertopo.com/topostore.html

Visit SuperTopo.com before each climb

There is much more beta for each climb in this guidebook available for free on the SuperTopo web site: http://www.supertopo.com. Visit the web site before your climb to be sure you have the latest information.

The web site offers additional free beta for each climb:
- photo galleries
- trip reports
- route conditions updates
- closures and rock fall warnings
- sign up for "route beta email alerts"

The web site is packed with general Yosemite info:
- free downloadable color topos
- road and weather conditions
- everything you need to know about staying in Yosemite
- good routes for first time Yosemite climbers
- general trip planning info

Yosemite Topropes

Chris McNamara

Yosemite has few easy routes and the polished granite and smooth cracks demand unfamiliar technique. Immediately jumping on a multi-pitch climb is generally a bad idea. Instead, spend a day or two at one of Yosemite's few toprope crags to get a feel for the rock and climbing style.

This guidebook contains enough topropes (listed below) to become acquainted with every technique—from steep hand jams to delicate friction slabs. Be aware that few toprope anchors in Yosemite can be walked to. Instead, you need to either lead an easier route to the side or the route itself to gain the anchors. Ideally, bring a ropegun—a confident climber who can lead the routes and set up the topropes.

In the table below, we have listed the toprope climbs contained in this guidebook along with key beta so you can plan which areas to visit.

Area	Route	Rating	Anchor Access	Technique
Swan Slab	Unnamed gully	5.1	walk	face
Church Bowl	Aunt Fanny's Pantry	5.5	climb route	chimney
Swan Slab	Swan Slab Chimney	5.5	climb route	chimney
Swan Slab	West Slabs	5.5-5.8	walk	face
Manure Pile Butt.	Fecophelia	5.6	scramble 3rd class	face, fists, hands
Swan Slab	Hanging Flake	5.6	climb route	hands
Swan Slab	Oak Tree Flake	5.6	climb 5.5	lieback
Swan Slab	Swan Slab Gully	5.6	climb route	face, fingers, hands
Church Bowl	Uncle Fanny	5.7	climb route	chimney
El Capitan Base	La Cosita Left	5.7	climb route	chimney, face
El Capitan Base	Pine Line	5.7	scramble 4th class	fingers
Knob Hill	Chicken Pie	5.7	walk then 5.5 move	fist, hands, lieback
Knob Hill	Potbelly	5.7	walk	fingers, hands
Sunnyside Bench	Jamcrack (first pitch)	5.7	climb route	hands
Swan Slab	Penelope's Problem	5.7	climb 5.6	hands
Swan Slab	Swan Slab Squeeze	5.7	climb 5.3	chimney
Swan Slab	Unnamed crack	5.7	climb 5.3	fingers, lieback
Swan Slab	Unnamed face	5.7	climb 5.6	face
Church Bowl	Church Bowl Lieback	5.8	climb route	lieback
El Capitan Base	Little John, Left	5.8	climb 5.8	fists, offwidth
El Capitan Base	Little John, Right	5.8	climb route	hands, fingers
Swan Slab	Penthouse cracks	5.8-5.11a	walk	fingers, hands, lb
El Capitan Base	La Cosita Right	5.9	climb 5.7	hands, lieback
Knob Hill	Unnamed	5.9	walk	fingers
Manure Pile Butt.	C.S. Concerto	5.9	walk	face, fingers
Sunnyside Bench	Lemon	5.9	climb 5.7	lieback
Swan Slab	Grants Crack	5.9	climb 5.5	fingers
Swan Slab	Unnamed crack	5.9	climb 5.3	fingers, lieback
Church Bowl	Deja Thorus	5.10a	climb 5.7	lieback
Church Bowl	Pole Position	5.10a	climb 5.7	face
Church Bowl	Revival	5.10a	climb 5.5	face, fingers
Swan Slab	Unnamed thin crack	5.10a	climb 5.5	face, fingers
Sunnyside Bench	Bummer	5.10c	climb 5.7	face, fingers, hands

Knob Hill

Approach time: **2 minutes**

Sun exposure: **mid-morning to afternoon**

Height of routes: **60-200'**

Chris McNamara

Knob Hill is a convenient introduction to longer Yosemite 5.7 and 5.8 pitches. The climbs are generally low angle and offer a mixture of straight-in cracks and wild face climbing on giant knobs. On most climbs, the cruxes come down low and are well-protected. A few of the routes are great topropes, but most of the pitches are too long. If it is your first time in Yosemite, you may want to stop at Swan Slab to get a feel for the rock and then head to Knob Hill to get in some longer moderate pitches. All but one anchor uses bolts or trees. The south-facing cliffs receive sun all day and are scorching in the summer, but often temperate during the winter.

Just for Starters, Sloth Wall, and Anti Ego Crack use the same tree anchor, which may cause problems if multiple parties are on the wall. Be prepared to wait for parties to finish or build intermediate anchors below and right of the tree. It is possible but impractical to toprope these climbs because they are so long. To set a toprope you will need to tie two ropes together and use numerous directionals. One toprope will tie up all three routes: Be considerate of other climbers at the crag.

Approach

From Camp 4, drive west to the Highway 120/140 junction. Turn right onto Highway 120, drive 1.8 miles, and park in the east-most paved pullout before the first Cascade Bridge over Cascade Creek. If that pullout is full, park in the larger paved pullout between the two bridges. From the east end of the east-most bridge, follow a climbers' trail up and right for 2 minutes to the base of the crags.

Descent

Descend Just for Starters, Sloth Wall, and Anti Ego Crack by rappelling from the tree with one 50m or 60m rope. Be sure to angle west toward the gully and be extra careful not to rappel off the end of the rope. If the tree anchor is in use by other parties, move left into the gully, belay off a tree, and then descend by scrambling down the gully.

To descend the other climbs, walk off from the last anchor.

History

I first saw Knob Hill when I was working for the NPS Road Crew on the road directly below. During a lunch break, I walked to the base and realized there were a couple of good climbs to do. I returned on the next days off with a guy from the east coast named Steve Miller and my late first wife Elsie (she died a few years later in a big boating accident on Mono Lake).

We did the "Anti Ego Crack" first, which was named because it was hard to have an ego trip over a climb with 20 feet of 5.7 right off the ground and then a big jug haul on a slab. Remember that this was a time when people like Jim Bridwell were pushing into unheard realms of difficulty and this climb went in the opposite direction.

The "Sloth Wall" was named because there were so many jugs you could climb hand over hand like a monkey. With climbers being more sloth-like in their habits and lifestyles "Sloth Wall" seemed appropriate.

We named "Just For Starters" because it looked like a fun little introductory route.

Unfortunately, somebody pulled hard on the initial holds, which we thought were solid, and they are gone. So instead of a 5.10c move it is now a 5.10a move. I imagine many people just French free past that move to get to the easier climbing above.

- *Jerry Anderson*

A. Unnamed   5.9★★

This climb offers an opportunity to enhance your finger jamming and footwork technique. While the crack takes decent protection, it is tricky to place and therefore the climb is seldom led. As you climb higher, the moves get harder as the finger locks and footholds are less positive. The crux bulge involves thin finger locks and sparse face holds over a bulge. To focus more on face technique, climb the 5.9 starting variation to the left.

B. Pot Belly   5.8★★★

FA: Bill Griffin and Bruce Price, 4/73.

Start on this climb, which offers great straight-in hand jamming. The first 10 feet are committing, technical, and require a spot if leading. The undercling roof start variation may feel easier depending on your granite face climbing experience. Either start is unprotected for 10 feet and most climbers will scramble to the bolt anchors and set a toprope. Above the tricky start, a splitter 5.7 hand crack offers sustained and enjoyable jamming (you will want to do at least a few laps on this upper section). Once comfortable on Pot Belly, try toproping the unnamed 5.9 to the left.

C. Just for Starters   5.10a★★★

FA: The Anderson Family, 1992.

After a bouldery and technical start, the climbing dramatically eases as large knobs appear. Because the crux is the first move, this is an easy way to break into the 5.10a realm. By Yosemite standards, this climb is well-protected at all the hard sections and runout once the climbing eases to 5.4.

Chris McNamara

D. Sloth Wall   5.7★★★★

FA: Steve Miller, Jerry Anderson, and Elsie Anderson, 10/72.

This climb takes you through moderate knob climbing paradise. A 5.7 crux down low is followed by enormous and comfortable knobs more reminiscent of the climbing gym than Yosemite. Cracks appear frequently to offer ample protection. Be sure to use many long slings down low to cut down on rope drag.

E. Anti Ego Crack   5.7★★★

FA: Steve Miller and Jerry Anderson, 10/72.

An exhilarating and strenuous start leads to low-angle wandering on big holds. At the start, lieback or fist jam as quickly and efficiently as possible. After 20 feet, the wide crack narrows and the climbing becomes dramatically easier. Almost all climbers avoid the optional second pitch.

F. Turkey Pie (aka Chicken Pie)   5.7★★

FA: Jerry Anderson, 7/73.

Turkey Pie will break you into 5.7 wide crack technique. A leaning lieback corner is followed by a gradually widening straight-in crack. Hand jams, fist jams, and a little offwidth technique are required. You can set a toprope with one 60m rope, but you will need to leave many directionals to keep a follower from swinging to the east.

Rack

A. Unnamed 5.9★★
nuts: 1 set
cams: 1 ea .4-2"

B. Pot Belly 5.8★★★
nuts: 1 set
cams: 1 ea .5-2.5"

C. Just for Starters 5.10a★★★
7 quickdraws

D. Sloth Wall 5.7★★★★
nuts: 1 set
cams: 1 ea .5-2.5"

E. Anti Ego Crack 5.7★★★
nuts: 1 set
cams: 1 ea .4-1.5"
       2 ea 1.75-3.5"

F. Turkey Pie 5.7★★
nuts: 1 set,
cams: 1 ea .5-1.5"
       2 ea 1.75-4"

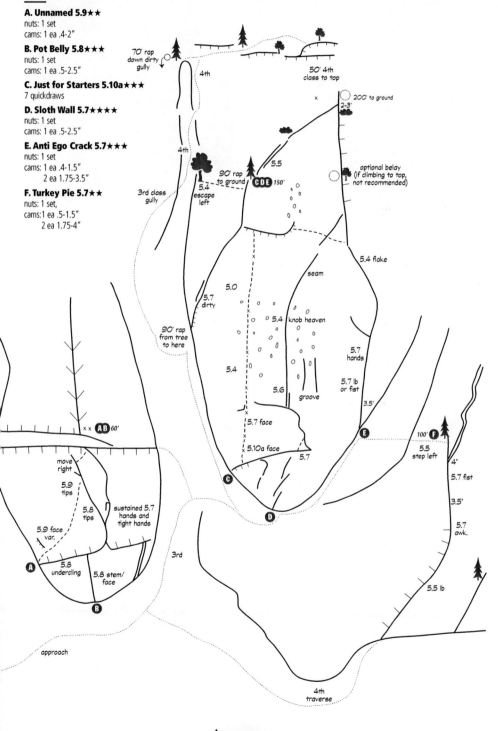

El Capitan Base

Approach time: **10 minutes**

Sun exposure: **late morning to afternoon**

Height of routes: **80-160'**

Generally when climbers think of El Capitan, aid walls and the most famous rock face in the world come to mind. Many Valley climbers don't notice the excellent free climbs along the base of the southwest face. While these climbs are not long and have similarities to routes elsewhere, the immense 3000-foot overhung headwall towering above sets it apart from the average crag. Because aid walls are above and sometimes start on the free climbs, there is increased danger of rockfall and dropped gear, and you should always wear a helmet. The free routes along the southwest base are known for slick rock and pure cracks requiring good technique.

The southwest base of El Cap gets hot in the summer and is best as a spring and fall destination. Even winter temperatures can be good, but the frequent massive icefall from the headwall makes winter climbing untenable. Several of the routes are popular, yet lines usually don't appear. However, if a party is aiding a wall and is starting up the free climb you're interested in, long waits can ensue.

Approach

From the triangle at El Cap Meadow, pick up the distinct trail that starts 50 feet west of the sign directing drivers to Highways 120, 140, and 41. Follow the trail a few hundred yards to a large clearing. When facing the wall, walk at 10 o'clock and pick up the distinct climbers' trail that eventually leads to a point 200 feet in front of the toe of the southeast buttress and the start of The Nose. From here, the trail diverges to skirt either the base of the southeast face or southwest face. Take the left fork leading to the base routes of the southwest face.

It is about a 0.25 mile and a 10- to 15-minute walk from the road to the toe of the Southeast Buttress and the start of The Nose.

Chris McNamara

1	Sacherer Cracker	4	Moby Dick, Center
2	La Cosita, Right	5	Salathé Wall (Pitch 1)
3	Little John, Right	6	Pine Line

Descent

Descend all climbs by rappelling. Reverse the approach.

History

Not many people hiked up to the base of El Cap back in the olden days. Why do it? The cliff was obviously not climbable, so why waste your energy? All this changed in 1958 after the first ascent of the Nose. Many climbers wandered up to gaze at the lower part of Harding's route and stroke the now-famous cliff.

A striking chimney route called The Slack was established even as Harding labored on the cliff above. Charlie Raymond, one of the first ascensionists and now a renowned glaciologist, told me recently that he had forgotten the origin of the name. "I think that my head has been filled up with too much science to remember anything important like climbing! There is definitely a story behind the name of The Slack, but for the life of me I can not remember it. I do not think that it is as simple as slot combined with crack." Within a few years this had become a popular route and, naturally, climbers soon saw other cracks and dihedrals leading to the top of minor slabs along the base of the great southwest flank of the monolith.

1962 was the breakthrough year. The weather was horrible during the spring, and long routes were out of the question. The base of El Cap, with its short approach and ultra-clean rock that dried quickly, became a favorite locale during breaks in the storms. April and May saw numerous first ascents, with perhaps the best being La Escuela, a four-pitch aid route up leaning dihedrals. This was the work of Yvon Chouinard and TM Herbert, who saw the route as ideal for beginning aid climbers (hence the name, which means "The School" in Spanish). Days later, Herbert and I did a fine, slippery lieback on tiny La Cosita, continuing the Spanish naming pattern—a trend that basically died with this route. Herb Swedlund and Penny Carr put up the spectacular Moby Dick, using a few aid pins—eliminated by Frank Sacherer within days. Three routes appeared on Delectable Pinnacle. Royal Robbins got into the act also; he and Jack Turner established a complex and classic route on the right side of Little John. The spring of 1962 was quite a time!

Within a few years all the various "pinnacles" at the base had been climbed, usually by three different routes: left side, center (often an aid route involving hairline cracks), and right side. Variations soon sprung up, an important one being the Sacherer Cracker, a two-pitch alternate to the lower part of The Slack. This 1964 route, done by Sacherer and Mike Sherrick, involved a 120-foot jamcrack that varied in width from one to six inches. At 5.10a, and difficult to protect (using bong-bongs), this was one of the bolder leads of the mid-1960s. Chouinard, greatly impressed with Sacherer's ability, wrote that he "always climbed on the verge of falling over backwards—using no more energy than was necessary to progress and rarely bothering to stop and place protection. Apparently his belayers have been so completely gripped they were unable to use a camera. I have not been able to find a single photograph of Sacherer on a lead!"

The next major event took place in 1973, when Steve Wunsch and Mark Chapman freed La Escuela. The lower two pitches,

once pure, strenuous aid, overnight became a different climb, one involving sustained liebacks at 5.11a. The pair eliminated about 35 aid points!

Another 11a route, Sparkling Give-away, vies for attention. Put up in 1991 by two big-wall tigers, Pete Takeda and Eric Kohl, this short line involves thin moves on the outer face of La Cosita.

All in all, the base of El Cap is a marvelous place, with aesthetic cracks, excellent belay ledges, easy rappels, and shaded slabs for picnics and spectators. Oh, yes, it's also a favorite haunt of rattlesnakes!

– Steve Roper

A. La Escuela   5.11b★★★★

FA: Yvon Chouinard and TM Herbert, 5/62.
FFA: Steve Wunsch and Mark Chapman, 1973.

Polished, sustained, and technical, La Escuela will 'school ya' in classic Yosemite liebacking. The protection is solid but can be difficult to place due to the sustained nature of the climb. Luckily the fall is clean. The crack seeps water early in the season so plan accordingly. A very classic route, but the grade keeps traffic down.

B. The Slack, Center   5.10d★★

FA: Chuck Pratt and Royal Robbins, 5/65.
FFA: Pat Ament and Larry Dalke, 1967.

Try this good double-rope toprope after doing Sacherer Cracker. The route has fingers in pin scars with technical stemming to a good 5.8 offwidth to a traversing chimney. Skip the chimney to reduce pendulum potential on toprope.

C. Sacherer Cracker   5.10a★★★★

FA: Frank Sacherer and Mike Sherrick, 1964.

An excellent, clean, widening crack up a steep wall, Sacherer Cracker is a beautiful climb. Don't underestimate the short 5.7 approach pitch, which is a polished flare that has spit out many a 5.11 climber. The crux is a section of slowly widening finger to hand cracks that rewards trusting, insecure jams and firing up to the first hand jam. Fifty feet of beautiful steep hands tests your endurance, and then a rest ledge lets you contemplate the 30 feet of off-hand/fist to the intimidating offwidth, which is the crux for most. A 1.25" cam in a horizontal crack and good chockstones at the base of the offwidth offer great pro, and the offwidth widens so quickly that huge cams don't help. Stick your right side in and make a few desperate moves (focus on bridging the outside foot). Sacherer Cracker often has a line, but consider La Cosita, Left and toproping Sparkling Give-Away.

D. The Mark of Art 5.10d★★★★

FA: Mark Chapman and Art Higbee, 1974.

Outstanding, burly endurance liebacking and off-fingers make The Mark of Art one of the testpiece Valley 5.10d climbs. The fact that it starts after the whole crux fingers to hand crack of Sacherer Cracker (and avoids its offwidth!) only makes this climb more appealing. Start from the bolts on top of Short but Thin to make one of the longest and best single pitches in the Valley.

E. Short but Thin 5.11b★★★

FA: Tobin Sorenson and John Bachar, 5/74.

Technical and strenuous, Short but Thin makes up for its length with fierce moves. Few people lead this, but thin cams and nuts protect it well. Toprope this climb by leading the polished 5.7 flare that begins Sacherer Cracker.

F. La Cosita, Left 5.7★★★★

FA: Bob Kamps, Galen Rowell, Dan Doody, Wally Upton, 6/62.

This is perhaps the best, and probably the steepest 5.7 pitch in the Valley. An intimidating, steep hand crack in a corner protects beautifully, but you climb via somewhat tricky but secure chimney. Higher, jugs appear, and a final awkward bulge tests you. A sketchy 5.9 offwidth/squeeze behind a flake takes off left after the first 20 feet, but is difficult to toprope safely.

G. Sparkling Give-away 5.11a★★

FA: Pete Takeda and Eric Kohl, 12/91.

Wild and challenging, this is a great toprope. The finger crack traverse rewards speed, and the crux can be done several ways—from a reachy undercling to a dicey mantel. Higher, staying left on reachy jugs is

easier, and staying right is excellent practice for hard, steep slab.

H. La Cosita, Right 5.9★★★★

FA: TM Herbert and Steve Roper, 5/63.

This is the Valley testpiece 5.9 lieback/finger crack. Incredibly slick liebacking off the ground sees many slips and falls, but completely bomber pro makes it safe. The trick is to find the lieback balance—the higher your feet, the more strenuous the climb—yet your feet will cut out at some point, and La Cosita teaches you how far you can push it on slick granite. Another lieback section higher is easier since you can get more purchase in the crack with your feet. From the bolted anchor you can toprope La Cosita, Left and Sparkling Give-away.

I. Little John, Left 5.8★★

FA: Dan Doody, Bob Kamps, Galen Rowell, Wally Upton, 8/62.

This slick, polished fist/tight offwidth crack is an excellent toprope after doing Little John, Right or a good lead in its own right. It is often somewhat obstructed by fixed lines.

J. Hardly Pinnacle 5.10d★★★★

FA: Dale Bard et al, 1972.

This is an outstanding and often overlooked climb. Beautiful, clean, steep liebacking is mixed with an intriguing crux of technical stemming. The first 25 feet has two options: either a burly lieback or a straight-up finger crack. Both are approximately the same difficulty depending on your strengths. Those willing to trust the normally fixed Heart Ledges lines and capable of safely ascending ropes, can ascend these lines, and pendulum right to set a toprope.

K. Little John, Right 5.8★★★★

FA: Jack Turner and Royal Robins, 4/62.

Three pitches of 5.8 make Little John, Right one of the most popular climbs in Yosemite. Many are in for a rude awakening on the first pitch—an awkward, polished chimney with tricky stemming awaits. Protection is good however, and it's fun to battle with new techniques. The second pitch is excellent, but many miss the traverse to the left and go too high. Study the topo and keep in mind that you are trying to get left. The last pitch has a fun, slick hand crack in a corner. From the bolts at the left end of the last pitch ledge, an 80-foot rappel reaches 3rd class ledges. But before you pack up, toprope Little John, Left—an excellent polished 5.8 offwidth. Do laps on this and you will get great training for the offwidths that you inevitably run into in Yosemite. The Heart Ledges fixed lines and rappel route come down here, and sometimes you are faced with people wrestling haulbags up the rappel. If that's the case, carefully look over the edge and find another bomber bolted anchor and rappel to the base (two ropes needed).

L. Moby Dick, Center   5.10a★★★★★

FA: Herb Swedlund and Penny Carr, 5/63.
FFA: Frank Sacherer and Steve Roper, 5/63.

While starting with a powerful and technical 5.10a finger crack, most climbers remember Moby Dick for the long battle above with a widening fist crack. For those with small hands, the top of Moby Dick is truly an offwidth, and hand stacking can allow secure rests. Those with large hands will love it, yet the finger crack crux may be correspondingly more difficult! Prepare and plan your pro for the start, as the crux is off the deck.

M. Ahab   5.10b★★★

FA: Frank Sacherer and Jim Bridwell, 9/64.

Ahab is a tough offwidth/flare. Rated 5.10b, it is a testament to Yosemite climbers of the 1960s. Ninety-nine out of a hundred 5.13 gym climbers would be completely shut down by this climb. Seldom led, toprope it from Moby Dick for practice at that most necessary Yosemite skill and the hallmark craft of any hard-core Valley climber: slick, flared offwidth.

N. Salathé Wall (Pitch 1 & 2)   5.10c★★★★★

The first pitches of the Salathé Wall are the start for several popular walls as well as Freeblast, a testpiece ten-pitch 5.11.

However, they also have one of the best, most sustained 5.10 finger cracks in the Valley. Long, thin fingers, fingers, double cracks, edges, and a thin hands crux make for an unforgettable lead. Good footwork helps make it through the 5.10 technical cruxes. The deceptively hard first 40 feet of the pitch is far to the left of the main crack, and many do this as a short approach pitch. However, the only good pro for an anchor is also far to the left, making it a problem if you place pro near the start of the finger crack (sustained 5.9 to 5.10a thin fingers). Therefore, the best way to safely climb this is to lead the start, traverse to the finger crack, get one or two good pieces, and go off belay, then pull your rope all the way through and toss back down. Then you can lead to the anchors over 100 feet above, and either have the follower risk a pendulum, or climb harder terrain directly up to the finger crack, and retrieve the gear on rappel. Before rappelling, consider the excellent and burly hands/lieback/offwidth next pitch. Only about 50 feet long and rated 5.8, it will prepare you for the grade encountered on longer routes.

O. Pine Line   5.7★★★★

FA: Jeff and Greg Schaffer, 7/66.

A fun, short 5.7 finger crack with pin scars, Pine Line starts from a huge ledge with great views. An excellent first lead or warm up, it protects with excellent nuts and a few cams, and is a great place for the overly cam-reliant novice climber to train with nuts. Several good 5.10d-11b slab/thin edge climbs can easily be toproped and are great training. The belay tree is a long way back from the edge and long slings can help extend the anchor past an intermediate bush. It is also an alternate start to the Nose and starts from a beautiful ledge.

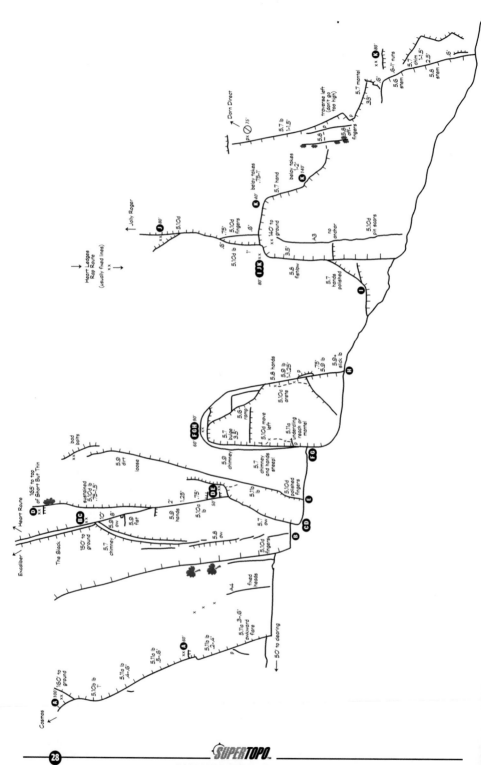

A. La Escuela 5.11b★★★★ nuts: many extra micro, thin, and sml, cams: many tiny to 2.5", esp. .5-.75"

B. The Slack, Left 5.10d★★ nuts: 1 set, cams: 1 ea 1-3", 2 ea .5-.75", 3.5-6", slings for chockstones

C. Sacherer Cracker 5.10a★★★★★ nuts: 1 set, cams: .5-3.5", can use large cams. (One 5" cam can be used for Pitch 1), slings for chockstones, other: big bros for offwidth.

D. The Mark of Art 5.10d★★★★★ nuts: 1 set, cams: .5-2.5", many extra .75-1.5" (If belaying on ledge, bring three 2.5-3.5" cams for belay)

E. Short but Thin 5.11b★★ nuts: 2 sets micro-sml, cams: lots of small/tiny

F. La Cosita, Left 5.7HHHH nuts: 1 set, cams: 6-4", extra 1-2"

G. Sparkling Give-away 5.11a★★ cams: 1 ea 3.5", optional .75", 3 draws

H. La Cosita, Right 5.9★★★ nuts: 1 set, cams: 1 ea .5-2", extra .5-2"

I. Little John, Left 5.8★★★ nuts: 1 set, cams: 1 set .6-2", 2 ea 2.5-3.5"

J. Hardly Pinnacle 5.10d★★★★ nuts: 1 set, include micro nuts/RPs, cams: 2 ea .5-1.25"

K. Little John, Right 5.8★★★★ nuts: 1 set, cams: .5-3", extra 1-2"

L. Moby Dick 5.10a★★★★★ nuts: 1 set thin-med, cams: 1 ea .5-4.5", extra 2.5-3.5"

M. Ahab 5.10b★★★ nuts: 1 set, cams: 1 set to 2", 2 ea 2.5-5"

N. Salathé Wall 5.10c★★★★★ nuts: 2 sets sml to med, 1 set large, cams: many .5-2", extra 2.5-4" if doing second pitch, many draws and slings

O. Pine Line 5.7★★★ nuts: 2 sets sml-med, cams: few .6-1", long slings for tree

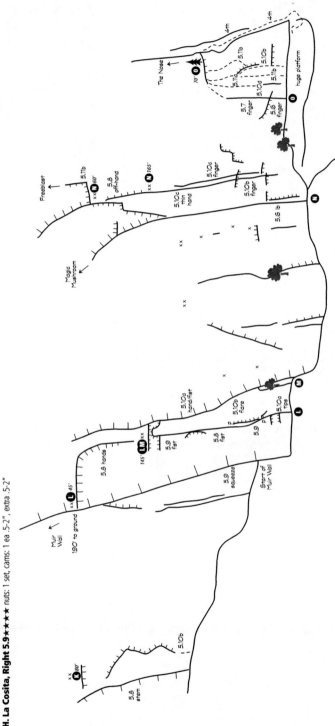

Manure Pile Buttress

Manure Pile Buttress hosts two of the Valley's premier multi-pitch climbs: Nutcracker and After Six. The 600 feet of clean and quality cracks are extremely popular due to the mellow approach and close proximity to Camp 4. Manure Pile Buttress is best known as the site of many climbers' first Yosemite multi-pitch ascent.

Approach

Heading west on Northside Drive toward El Capitan, take a right into a picnic area 1.6 miles west of Camp 4. From the northeast end of the parking lot, just behind the bathroom, follow a well-traveled trail northeast for a few hundred yards to the base of Manure Pile Buttress. After Six is the 150-foot right-facing corner seen immediately upon reaching the rock face. Nutcracker begins 200 feet to the right (east). A short scramble leads to a ledge with a large tree, a 20-foot-tall dead stump, and large dihedrals extending from either side.

Descent

From the top of the climbs, move to the northwest and follow a worn scramble/trail up a short distance then down and northwest for 200 feet of 3rd and 4th class to a climbers' trail. Follow this trail as it switchbacks to the base of After Six.

Nutcracker III 5.8★★★★★

Time to climb route:	**2-4 hours**
Approach time:	**5 minutes**
Descent time:	**25 minutes**
Sun exposure:	**late morning to afternoon**
Height of route:	**600'**

Nutcracker is a classic due to its interesting history, easy approach, and five great pitches of perfect Yosemite granite. Climbing the route, one will encounter liebacking, hand jamming, finger jamming, delicate smearing, and an exposed mantel crux. Nutcracker is a good increase in challenge following After Six and After Seven.

History

The first ascent of the most popular Valley climb ever was a historic breakthrough, for it was one of the first routes done solely with nuts. Even though Royal Robbins had climbed twice in England by 1966, he hadn't fully embraced nut use for Yosemite. Royal wrote in June 1966: "I think we can learn a lot from the British, and I see a place in the U. S. for the concept that placing a lot of pitons is not good style and also for the use of nuts at places like Tahquitz, where years of placing and removing pitons have worn the cracks so much as to change the routes." In 1967, Robbins found a magnificent climb at Manure Pile Buttress to test his idea that nuts might be appropriate for Yosemite after all and named his new route, in his usual punning mode, Nutcracker Sweet. Within months, those ignorant of Tchaikovsky had shortened the name simply to its first word, and that's how it has been for three decades.

An unwritten rule, obeyed by virtually everyone, was that no piton would ever be driven into this route. Many a Valley climber learned how effective nuts could be (this was long before camming devices were available) and left pitons and hammers in camp. Robbins, the king of the Big Walls, had once again proved that he was the guiding light of 1960s Valley climbing.

Climbers soon swarmed up other routes and variations on Manure Pile Buttress, and the place became a mandatory stop on everyone's itinerary. You also won't see many piton scars, those dreadful excavations still so visible on the popular routes of the early 1960s. Thanks Royal!

– Steve Roper

Strategy

Start early as this route is extremely popular. Nutcracker usually has climbers on every pitch, creating the prospect of being stuck behind slower parties. If you arrive at the base and find a long line, consider climbing Fecophilia (5.6) and toproping C. S. Concerto (5.9) to warm up while waiting. All belays require gear.

The crux of this climb is the exposed 5.8 mantel on the final pitch. Some climbers use small holds above and to the left to avoid the direct mantel move. Take time to set good protection here. Keep a close belay—falls from this move have resulted in broken ankles.

The 5.9 polished fingers variation on the first pitch offers another way to pass parties.

In the summer, the route gets sun nearly all day, so bring plenty of water. Afternoon winds or storms are not uncommon, especially in the spring and fall.

If you are feeling motivated, head back to the base and climb After Six or After Seven.

Retreat

Carry two 50m or 60m ropes for retreating this route. To retreat from the second belay, rappel either the 5.9 variation or the rappel route on the face. Above the second belay, it is more difficult to retreat and will require leaving gear.

Nutcracker		Pitch				
		1	2	3	4	5
Free difficulty	≥5.10					
	5.9					
	5.8	●			●	●
	5.7			●		
	5.6					
	≤5.5	●				

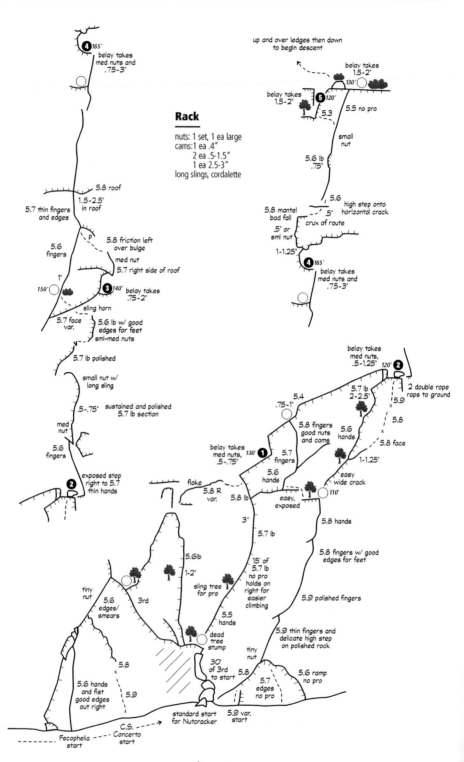

Rack

nuts: 1 set, 1 ea large
cams: 1 ea .4"
2 ea .5-1.5"
1 ea 2.5-3"
long slings, cordalette

up and over ledges then down
to begin descent

belay takes
1.5-2"
5 120'   5.5 no pro

belay takes
1.5-2"   130'

5.3

small
nut

5.6 lb
.75"

5.6

high step onto
horizontal crack

5.8 mantel   .5'   crux of route
bad fall   .5' or
sml nut

1-1.25"

4 165'
belay takes
med nuts and
.75-3'

belay takes
med nuts and
.75-3'

4 165'

5.8 roof

1.5-2.5"
in roof

5.7 thin fingers
and edges

5.6
fingers

5.8 friction left
over bulge

med nut

5.7 right side of roof

1"   150'   **3** 140'   belay takes
.75-2"

sling horn

5.7 face
var.

5.6 lb w/ good
edges for feet
sml-med nuts

5.7 lb polished

small nut w/
long sling

.5-.75"   sustained and polished
5.7 lb section

med
nut

5.6
fingers

exposed step
right to 5.7
thin hands

2

flake

5.8 R
var.   5.8 lb

3'

5.7 lb

5.6lb

1-2"

sling tree
for pro

5.5
hands

dead
tree
stump

30'
of 3rd
to start

tiny
nut

5.6
edges/
smears   3rd

5.8

5.6 hands
and fist
good edges
out right   5.9

tiny
nut

5.8   5.7
edges
no pro

belay takes
med nuts,
.5-1.25"   120'   **2**

5.7 lb
2-2.5"   2 double rope
raps to ground

5.4
.75-1"   5.9

5.8 fingers
good nuts
and cams   5.6
hands   5.8

5.8 face

belay takes
med nuts,   130'   **1**   5.7
.5-.75"   fingers   1-1.25"

easy
wide crack

5.6
hands

easy,
exposed   110'

5.8 hands

5.8 fingers w/ good
edges for feet

15' of
5.7 lb
no pro
holds on
right for
easier
climbing

5.9 polished fingers

5.9 thin fingers and
delicate high step
on polished rock

5.6 ramp
no pro

standard start
for Nutcracker   5.9 var.
start

C.S.
Concerto
start

Fecophelia
start

After Six III 5.7★★★★★

Time to climb route: **2-4 hours**

Approach time: **5 minutes**

Descent time: **25 minutes**

Sun exposure: **late morning to afternoon**

Height of route: **600'**

With six pitches of moderate cracks and a short approach, After Six is the most popular 5.7 route in Yosemite. A step up in difficulty from Munginella, the climbing is varied, fun, and amazingly consistent in difficulty throughout the route. It has a little bit of everything but is not overwhelming.

History

It seems likely that we'll never know who discovered Manure Pile Buttress as a climbing objective. Back in the mid-1960s a dirt track led directly to its base from the main Valley road below the Lower Brother, but this side road seemed to lead only to a gigantic pile of horseshit, for this is where flunkies from the Valley stables deposited it, far from tourists with sensitive noses. Manure Pile Buttress was also known as Ranger Rock, and Camp 4 climbers in the 1960s knew that rangers often practiced their rescue techniques there. What with the stench and the possibility of encountering authority, local Valley hotshots stayed far away. Yet it's likely that weekenders played around on the lower section, a non-threatening beginners' area.

The first complete route, as far as is known, was the brainchild of Yvon Chouinard, who in June 1965 took a beautiful eastern climber, Ruth Schneider, up the most obvious line, named After Six since that's when they started (six in the evening, one might add, not the morning). This climb attracted immediate attention for two reasons: it was fun, and it was one of the few Valley climbs where the belayer could sit in the front seat of a car. After Six soon became the most sociable of climbs; beer-guzzling spectators could hurl insults upward without even shouting.

Chouinard returned in 1967 and did a much harder route, just left of After Six. This he accomplished with a handsome Scottish lass, Joy Herron. Chouinard named the route Jump for Joy, a nice pun made even nicer by the rumor, neither confirmed nor denied, that a breathtaking sexual act had occurred on the first big ledge.

- Steve Roper

Strategy

Get a really early start to be first on the route, or to beat the summer heat. After Six is the first multi-pitch experience for many climbers. However, like any climb in Yosemite, it is not to be underestimated, and some pitches could prove treacherous to the novice leader, especially Pitch 3.

The high traffic has polished the first pitch corner to the point where the original 5.6 rating has been bumped to 5.7. This pitch is challenging due to the sustained, awkward jamming with slick feet. However, excellent protection is available at all points, and the climbing is not to be feared.

Higher on the route, the moves are easier but occasionally not as well-protected. On Pitch 3, the psychological crux, the leader must face climb on the left arête of an exposed wide crack that has relatively poor protection.

For those comfortable at the grade, do both After Six and Nutcracker for an excellent day of climbing.

Retreat

Rappel After Six from the first pitch with two ropes. Higher on the route, leave gear, rappel slings around trees, or consider the somewhat dicey 4th class traverse/descent off left of Pitch 1 and Pitch 4. In a storm, the route will get very wet, but the danger of lightning strikes is relatively low.

After Six		Pitch 1	2	3	4	5	6
Free difficulty	≥5.10						
	5.9						
	5.8						
	5.7	●					
	5.6		●	●	●	●	●
	≤5.5		●				

Rack

nuts: 1-2 sets
cams: 2 ea .5-2.5"
     1 ea 3"

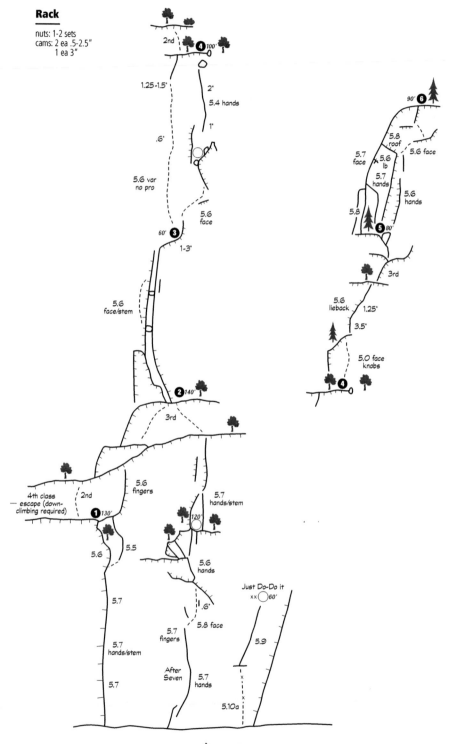

2nd **4** 100'

1.25-1.5'

2"
5.4 hands

1"

.6"

5.6 var
no pro

5.6
face

60' **3**

1-3"

5.6
face/stem

2 140'

3rd

4th class
escape (down-
climbing required)

2nd

1 130'

5.6
fingers

5.7
hands/stem

120'

5.6
hands

5.6   5.5

5.7

5.7
hands/stem

5.7

5.7
fingers

After
Seven

5.7
hands

.6"

5.8 face

Just Do-Do it
xx ◯ 60'

5.9

5.10a

90' **6**

5.8
roof

5.7
face

5.6
lb

5.6 face

5.7
hands

5.6
hands

5.8

5 80'

3rd

5.6
lieback   1.25'

3.5'

5.0 face
knobs

4

Swan Slab

Approach time: **2 minutes**

Sun exposure: **morning to afternoon**

Height of routes: **30-100'**

Conveniently located within a 5-minute walk of Camp 4, Swan Slab offers the highest concentration of short, moderate routes in Yosemite. Its not a single slab as the name implies, but a broad cliff composed of many one and two-pitch climbs ranging from near vertical cracks to slabby face climbs. The area offers everything from 5.1 to 5.11 with emphasis on the 5.6-5.8 difficulty range. Most climbs are 30 to 60 feet tall and make great topropes. Some topropes are set by scrambling to the top of the climbs. In most cases, however, you will need to do some leading on an easier climb nearby to set a toprope. Most climbs can be led with the following gear: one set of nuts, one set of cams .6-3", and some long slings. We note in the text when more gear is needed.

The south-facing cliff gets sun all day with perfect temperatures in the spring and fall. During the summer, the temperatures are enjoyable in the shade, but only tolerable in the sun. In the winter, if the routes are in the sun, the temperatures are usually good.

Approach

Swan Slab is located about halfway between Camp 4 and the Lower Yosemite Falls parking area. Park in Camp 4 and walk northeast 200 feet to the wide semi-paved trail. Walk east for a few minutes until directly below Swan Slab.

Descent

Rappel most routes with one 50m or 60m rope. On a few climbs you may want to walk off (see topo).

A. Penthouse Cracks   5.8-5.11a★★

These four cracks can be toproped from the same two-bolt anchor that you can walk to. They are perfect for building finger crack, hand crack, and lieback technique.

Chris McNamara

B. West Slabs   5.6-5.8★★

This is a great toprope to learn 5.1-5.8 slab technique. There are at least five variations from the anchor, which get progressively harder moving right to left. The tree anchor can be walked to and should be backed up with gear.

C. Unnamed Gully   5.1★

This route is great for children and first time climbers.

D. Unnamed flared crack   5.8★★

This steep and powerful climb is usually climbed as a boulder problem. The route traverses right under a roof and is difficult to toprope.

E. Unnamed crack   5.7★★

This short toprope is great for working on challenging moves without having to worry about exposure. You may need to set a directional from the tree anchor.

F. Unnamed crack   5.9★★

A bouldery start leads to sustained but short lieback moves. Do laps on this climb to refine your lieback technique.

G. Unnamed squeeze chimney   5.7★★

A good practice squeeze chimney that gets harder the higher you climb. Use foot-bridging technique and face out from the wall. Set a toprope by scrambling up 3rd class and some 5.3 to the anchors of D, E, and F. Then climb a few more moves to where the gaping crack constricts and set an anchor with 1-3" cams. The crack is seldom led because it requires 7-10" gear.

H. Unnamed chimney/gully   5.5★

This is an unaesthetic climb that does offer some good chimney practice. If you face the back of the chimney you will find that the climbing is awkward. Face outward with your back to the main wall if you want to practice true chimney technique. This offers the easiest anchor access for Oak Tree Flake or Grants Crack.

I. Oak Tree Flake   5.6★★★

5.6 jamming leads to a fun lieback flake. If led, the 3-4.5" cam placements are hard to see. This climb is frequently soloed and is conducive to laps. When setting a toprope, use the bolt anchors, but bring slings and cams to set a directional.

J. Grant's Crack   5.9★★★

This is a great first 5.9 crack lead or toprope. Do a few laps to build finger crack technique. Set the toprope by climbing the 5.5 chimney or Oak Tree Flake.

K. Unnamed thin crack   5.10a★★

This toprope develops thin crack and face technique. Set the toprope anchor by climbing the 5.5 chimney or Oak Tree Flake and continuing up a short 5.4 crack.

Chris McNamara

L. Unnamed thin crack   5.10c★★

A harder variation to K that requires more face technique. Set the toprope anchor by climbing the 5.5 chimney or Oak Tree Flake and continuing up a short 5.4 crack.

M. Penelope's Problem   5.7★★

Steep and short 5.7 hand jams lead to a short traverse to Swan Slab gully. Set protection before the traverse. To set a toprope, either climb the route or climb Swan Slab Gully. Beware that Swan Slab Gully is so awkward that some climbers may actually find Penelope's Problem easier despite its harder rating.

N. Swan Slab Gully   5.6★

An awkward and unaesthetic route that offers some interesting stemming, jamming, and face move challenges.

O. Unnamed face   5.7★★★

Bouldering thin friction moves leads to progressively easier climbing. Set a toprope by climbing Hanging Flake. For the 5.8 variation, start to the left and make a few bouldery face moves before eventually joining the upper part of the main route.

P. Hanging Flake   5.6★★

A short and fun introduction to hand jamming. The anchor is fractured and loose so set gear in many locations and equalize.

Chris McNamara

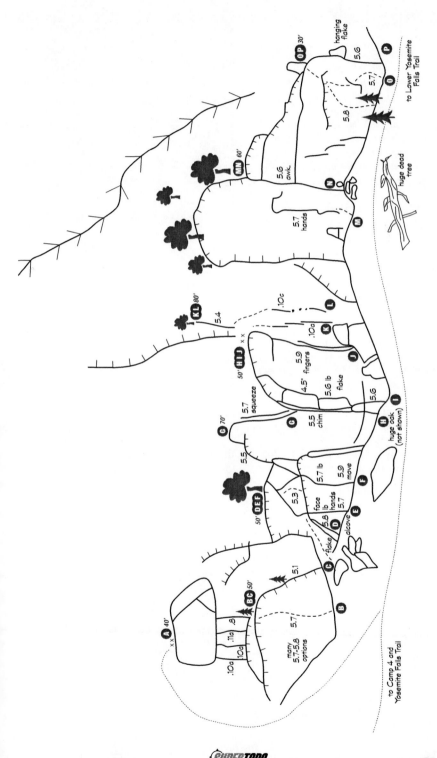

Five Open Books

Five Open Books provides a number of terrific climbs with relatively easy access. All routes described here are large right-facing corners (known as "open books") that face southeast and receive direct sun from morning to mid-day. In the spring and fall, ideal climbing temperatures are present from morning to mid-afternoon. During the summer, it is best to climb later in the day when the routes have gone into the shade.

WARNING: Never climb any of these routes without helmets due to the frequent climber-caused rockfall. Don't even stand at the base of a route without a helmet.

Approach

Munginella and Commitment
Park in the Lower Yosemite Fall parking area. Walk north 100 yards on the paved Lower Yosemite Fall Trail until it splits. Turn 90 degrees to the left (west) and locate a climbers' trail marked by a carabiner post. Follow the obvious trail marked by a total of four carabiner posts. The fourth post is within 15 feet of the wall and the start of Munginella. To reach Commitment, either climb the Munginella third class and move way right or skirt the base of the wall down then up. 100 feet of third class leads to the start of Commitment.

Selaginella
The recommended approach for Selaginella is to climb Munginella or Commitment.

As an alternate approach, follow the approach description above for Munginella and Commitment. From the fourth and last carabiner post, head west along the cliff to the streambed. Hike the streambed to a point where the slabs can be climbed (4th class in early season when wet, 3rd class when dry). Move east (right) along the top of the slabs, following the well-traveled climbers' trail east a few hundred yards to the base of the route.

1	Munginella	3	Selaginella
2	Commitment	4	Yosemite Falls Trail

Descent

Munginella and Commitment
Walk west along a trail for 200 yards until you reach the open slabs area. Continue west across the slabs to a 3rd/4th class descent trail. Consider rappelling this section when wet. The rappel can be done with one 50m rope by staying a bit to the left at the bottom. Below the slabs, follow the trail east and downward along the buttress, then slightly back uphill to the large, open flat area below the start of the routes.

Below the open slabs there is an alternate descent trail that continues down and west that is slightly worse than the descent option described above.

Selaginella
Head to the Yosemite Falls Trail. Go down this trail (west), reaching the Valley floor at Camp 4 (about one mile). From Camp 4, walk back east to the Lower Yosemite Fall parking area (leaving nothing at the base of the route will save you from hiking up again; the best option is to walk from Camp 4 to begin with if you are intending to do Selaginella).

Munginella 5.6★★★★

Time to climb route:	**2-3 hours**
Approach time:	**15 minutes**
Descent time:	**25 minutes**
Sun exposure:	**morning to afternoon**
Height of route:	**350'**

The route name, Munginella, no longer accurately describes this climb. Every pitch features clean cracks and quality climbing. Although this is one of Yosemite's easier multi-pitch climbs, the route is sustained and challenging. Don't lead it unless you are a solid 5.7 climber.

History

Climbers have always appreciated short approaches, so it's not surprising that the area around Lower Yosemite Fall attracted attention in the 1960s. Only minutes from Camp 4 lay a wealth of possible routes on the various tiers of cliffs. One trouble: these cliffs were not exactly composed of pristine granite. Trees, bushes, munge, loose dark rock—you name it, these cliffs had it. In a valley renowned for its sparkling white granite, this area was an aberration. But let's not forget that approach!

Wally Reed and Jim Posten were the first to explore the area. Five major open books could be seen on the first tier of cliffs, off to the left of the waterfall. But the next tier above looked cleaner, so they proceeded up to it and established a fine 5.7 route, later upticked to 5.8. Reed, fascinated by botany, named the climb Selaginella, after a fernlike plant found on the route.

In June 1966, Jim Bridwell and Phil and Dave Bircheff investigated the lowest tier

and climbed the 5.9 Commitment, the second-from-the-left of the Five Open Books. The classic curving lieback on the third pitch was...committing! That same summer Tom Fender and an unknown partner (cleverly called "Vic Tishous" in subsequent guidebooks) did the far-left book, the now-popular Munginella. The name, of course, is a takeoff on Selaginella, commemorating the vast amounts of vegetation encountered. Today, all three routes are clear of munge and brush.

– Steve Roper

Strategy

For some, finding the start is the crux of the climb. Munginella is the left-most of the Five Open Books. However, there is a huge 100-foot-tall right-facing corner to the left of Munginella that suckers in many climbers because it is located above the start of the 3rd class. Remember that the 3rd class approach to the first pitch diagonals up and right.

Pitch 2, the crux, requires a few committing face moves with protection below your feet. Use many long slings on this pitch to avoid rope drag.

At the last belay, take extreme care not to send rocks onto climbers below.

For those comfortable with leading sustained 5.8 wide cracks involving tricky routefinding, consider continuing up Selaginella for an additional four pitches of 5.7 and 5.8 climbing.

Retreat

The route can be rappelled with one 60m rope or two 50m ropes. The first belay has fixed slings for rappelling. Up higher, you will need to leave gear in order to retreat.

More at SuperTopo.com

Before climbing this route, see what other climbers have to say about the rock fall danger so that you can evaluate the risk for yourself.
www.supertopo.com/rockclimbing/route.html?r=yofimung

		Pitch		
Munginella		**1**	**2**	**3**
Free difficulty	≥5.10			
	5.9			
	5.8			
	5.7			
	5.6	●	●	♀
	≤5.5			

Commitment 5.9★★★

Time to climb route: **2-3 hours**

Approach time: **15 minutes**

Descent time: **25 minutes**

Sun exposure: **morning to afternoon**

Height of route: **350'**

This climbs warms you up with two straightforward pitches then blasts you with a tricky and memorable crux. Although this is a first 5.9 Valley route for many climbers, there is nothing easy about Commitment. The route's wild crux is, well, committing.

Strategy

Finding the start is difficult. Keep in mind that Commitment is the second from the left book of the Five Open Books and starts after third class scrambling. If you start up a right-facing corner right off the ground, then you are off route.

The third pitch is the clear crux of the route. It involves committing 5.9 lieback moves above solid protection. The route tops out on a sandy ledge; please be conscious of dropping rocks and dirt on parties below.

The east-facing wall gets sun early in the day, making it a great spring and fall climb. In the summer, start in the afternoon once the route has gone into the shade. During the late spring and early summer, mist from Yosemite Falls occasionally graces the climb. Once finished, consider continuing up Selaginella for four additional pitches of 5.7 and 5.8 climbing.

Retreat

Retreat requires two 50m ropes and gets more difficult as you climb higher due to the roof systems traversing right.

Commitment		Pitch 1	2	3
Free difficulty	≥5.10			
	5.9			●
	5.8	●		
	5.7		●	
	5.6			
	≤5.5			

Selaginella 5.8★★★

Time to climb route: **2-3 hours**

Approach time: **1.5 hours**

Descent time: **45 minutes-1 hour**

Sun exposure: **morning to afternoon**

Height of route: **550'**

With features ranging from lieback cracks and steep faces to offwidths and chimneys, Selaginella requires a full arsenal of climbing techniques. Prepare for committing and sustained 5.7 and 5.8 cracks up to the route's great final crux. Because of the sustained wide cracks and tricky routefinding, this route is recommended for the more experienced 5.8-5.9 leader.

Strategy

Most parties approach the route by climbing Munginella or Commitment, which, when linked with Selaginella, makes for seven pitches of moderate climbing.

There are two starting variations. The recommended right start has many wide cracks. An alternate start to the left features meandering climbing and bad rope drag but is free of wide cracks. As with all climbs at the Five Open Books, the ledge at the top of this route is loose. Be mindful of dislodging rocks onto climbers below. In addition, the Yosemite Falls Trail crosses directly above this route so there is a slight hazard of rocks or dropped items from hikers along this path.

Retreat

The route can be rappelled from a number of areas along the climb using two 50m ropes. Retreat gets more difficult as you climb higher on the traversing route.

Selaginella		Pitch 1	2	3	4
Free difficulty	≥5.10				
	5.9				
	5.8			●	●
	5.7	●	●		
	5.6				
	≤5.5				

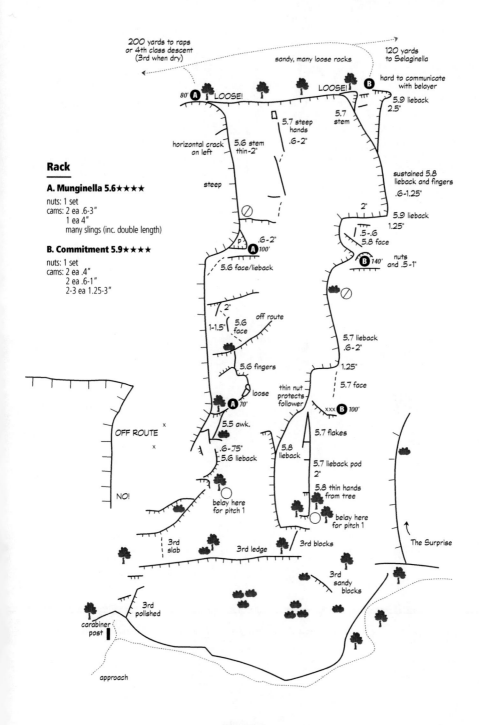

200 yards to raps
or 4th class descent
(3rd when dry)

sandy, many loose rocks

120 yards
to Selaginella

hard to communicate
with belayer

80' Ⓐ LOOSE!

LOOSE! Ⓑ

5.9 lieback
2.5"

5.7 steep
hands
.6-2"

5.7
stem

horizontal crack
on left

5.6 stem
thin-2"

5.7
stem

Rack

A. Munginella 5.6 ★★★★

nuts: 1 set
cams: 2 ea .6-3"
      1 ea 4"
      many slings (inc. double length)

B. Commitment 5.9 ★★★★

nuts: 1 set
cams: 2 ea .4"
      2 ea .6-1"
      2-3 ea 1.25-3"

steep

sustained 5.8
lieback and fingers
.6-1.25"

2"

5.9 lieback
1.25"

.5-.6
5.8 face

.6-2"
P Ⓐ 100'

5.6 face/lieback

Ⓑ 140'

nuts
and .5-1"

2"
1-1.5"

5.6
face

off route

5.7 lieback
.6-2"

5.6 fingers

1.25"

5.7 face

Ⓐ 70'

loose

thin nut
protects
follower

xxx Ⓑ 100'

OFF ROUTE

x

x

5.5 awk.

5.7 flakes

.6-.75"
5.6 lieback

5.8
lieback

5.7 lieback pod
2"

NO!

belay here
for pitch 1

5.8 thin hands
from tree

belay here
for pitch 1

The Surprise

3rd
slab

3rd ledge

3rd blocks

3rd
sandy
blocks

3rd
polished

carabiner
post

approach

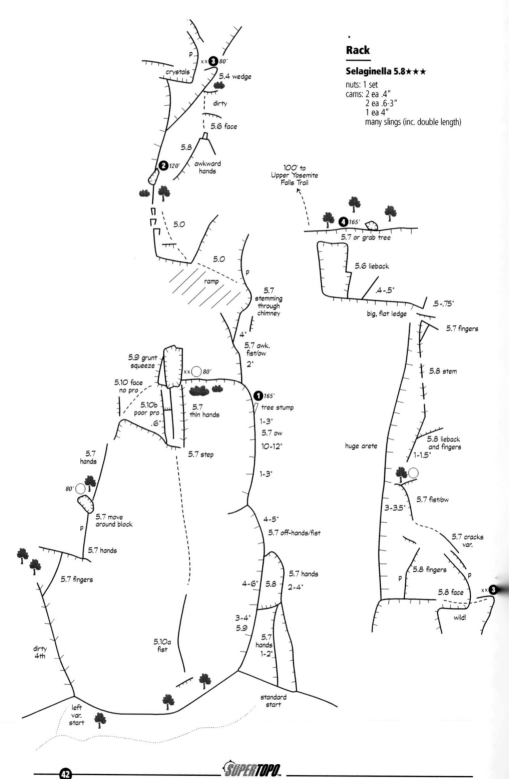

Rack

Selaginella 5.8★★★

nuts: 1 set
cams: 2 ea .4"
2 ea .6-3"
1 ea 4"
many slings (inc. double length)

P
xx ❸ 80'
crystals
5.4 wedge
dirty
5.6 face
5.8
❷ 120'
awkward
hands

100' to
Upper Yosemite
Falls Trail

5.0

5.0

ramp
P

5.7
stemming
through
chimney

4"

5.7 awk.
fist/ow

2"

5.9 grunt
squeeze
xx ◯ 80'

5.10 face
no pro

5.10b
poor pro
.6"

5.7
thin hands

5.7
hands

80' ◯

5.7 move
around block
P

5.7 hands

5.7 fingers

dirty
4th

5.10a
fist

left
var.
start

❶ 165'
tree stump

1-3"

5.7 ow

10-12"

1-3"

4-5"

5.7 off-hands/fist

5.7 hands
4-6" 5.8 2-4"

3-4"
5.9

5.7
hands
1-2"

standard
start

❹ 165'
5.7 or grab tree

5.6 lieback

.4-.5"

5-.75"
big, flat ledge

5.7 fingers

5.8 stem

5.8 lieback
and fingers
1-1.5"

huge arete

3-3.5"
5.7 fist/ow

5.7 cracks
var.

5.8 fingers
P
P

5.8 face
xx ❸

wild!

5.7 step

Sunnyside Bench

Approach time: **15 minutes**

Sun exposure: **morning to afternoon**

Height of routes: **160'**

East of the (seasonally) thundering Lower Yosemite Fall, Sunnyside Bench features a great introduction to moderate and advanced crack climbing. The area features cracks in the finger to hands range with difficulties of 5.7 to 5.10. Most of the routes are easy to toprope. All routes face south and receive sun until the late afternoon. During the summer, climb early in the morning or after 5 p.m. when the routes go into the shade. Be aware that the mosquitoes can be especially nasty during June.

Approach

From the Lower Yosemite Fall parking area, 0.3 miles east of Camp 4, walk north on the paved trail toward the fall. Cross the bridge at the base of the fall and continue east along the trail for 100 yards. At a point where the trail comes close to the base of a cliff (Sunnyside Bench), move left (north) to a climbers' trail paralleling the cliff face. Follow the switchbacks for 200 feet. The Jamcrack is the obvious hand crack leading to a ledge 80 feet up. Left of Jamcrack, Lazy Bum and Bummer are the two thin cracks leading to the same ledge. Twenty feet left of these is the right-facing steep lieback flake of Lemon.

Descent

Descend all routes by rappelling. Two ropes are required to swing and set a toprope on Lemon, and to descend from Pitch 2 of Lazy Bum. Otherwise, a single rope and two rappels suffice to descend.

History

Where to take girls climbing? This was the admittedly sexist question for climbers of a much earlier generation—mine, in fact. Not that we had anything special in mind, of course, but it would be fun to find an easy

Todd Snyder

| 1 | Bummer | 3 | Jamcrack |
| 2 | Lazy Bum | | |

route, show off a little, and maybe even have a swim at the end. And what better place for this than Sunnyside Bench, with magnificent pools atop it. Even the name was bound to attract the fair sex. Not a "wall," not a "crack," but a bench. And presumably a sunny one at that.

No one knows who first discovered the pools atop Lower Yosemite Fall, but it could well have been John Muir, known for prowling around this area (he lived for a few years only 150 yards from the waterfall). In any case, the Bench was well known to climbers of the 1930s. A class 4 route a few hundred yards right of the waterfall was the most direct way up, but one could get onto the Bench via an even easier way, much further east.

The routes Sunnyside is now renowned for began fairly late. Jamcrack was done with a bit of aid by Kim Schmitz and Loyd Price in 1967. Schmitz returned shortly thereafter to free the route—at 5.9—with Jim Madsen.

– Steve Roper

A. Lemon   5.9★★

FA: Dave Sessions and Scott Burke, 8/79.

This route is much more appealing as a toprope. Toprope by swinging left on a double-rope rappel from the Pitch 2 anchors on Jamcrack. It is difficult to reach from the Pitch 1 anchors. The route continues half a pitch, but is very dirty and seldom done.

B. Bummer   5.10c★★★

FA: Bruce Morris, Scott Cole, and Peter Thurston, 10/77.

The first pitch features good climbing with a desperate crux. It is usually toproped after climbing Pitch 1 of Jamcrack. Pitch 2 has excellent polished 5.9 face climbing, but is runout and easily toproped from the Pitch 2 anchors of Jamcrack.

C. Lazy Bum   5.10d★★★

FA: Eric Beck and Steve Williams, 1971.
FFA: Chris Falkenstein et al, 1972.

Pitch 1 is an excellent finger crack/lieback that is usually toproped after climbing Pitch 1 of Jamcrack. Powerful finger crack start (shared with Bummer) leads to a positive and technical traverse right. Beautiful, sustained, steep fingers leads to a thin and delicate 10-foot crux of liebacking (difficult to place pro at crux). Pitch 2 is an excellent technical and endurance challenge. Beware of the munge that is sometimes present if the pitch has not been recently climbed.

D. Jamcrack   5.9★★★

FA: Loyd Price and Kim Schmitz, 1967.
FFA: Kim Schmitz and Jim Madsen.

Because of the solid pro and short crux, the first pitch of Jamcrack is the first crack lead for many Yosemite newcomers. Consequently, be prepared to wait in line unless starting early in the morning. As the name indicates, this is the perfect crack to enhance your hand and finger jamming technique.

With three or more people, it is easy to set a toprope on the first pitch, then have a novice leader and belayer "lead" the first pitch, backed up with the toprope. If you do this, be sure to set a two-piece equalized directional before the traverse to the bolts. A belay can be set in the thin crack 10 feet right of the bolts (start of Pitch 2 of Lazy Bum) if crowds are occupying the bolts. Linking the two pitches is not recommended due to the 20-foot traverse on the ledge.

Don't pass up the chance to toprope two excellent 5.10 cracks: Bummer and Lazy Bum. In addition, Lemon, a short excellent 5.9 lieback can be toproped.

With one 50m or 60m rope you can rappel all pitches except for the second pitch of Lazy Bum, which requires two ropes to descend.

A. Lemon 5.9★★ nuts: 1 set, cams: 2 ea .75-3"
B. Bummer 5.10c★★★ nuts: 1 set, cams: 1 ea .5-2"
C. Lazy Bum 5.10d★★★ nuts:1 set, cams: 1 ea .5-2"
D. Jamcrack 5.9★★★ nuts: 1 set, cams: 1 ea .4-3"

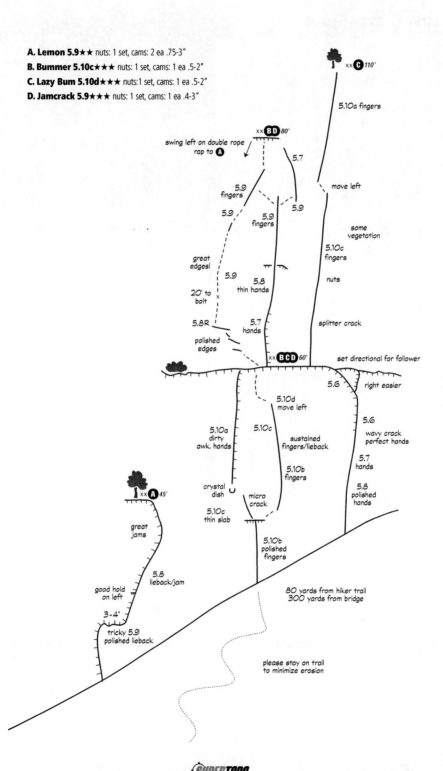

xx **C** 110'

5.10a fingers

swing left on double rope
rap to **A**

xx **B D** 80'

5.7

move left

5.9
fingers

5.9

5.9

5.9
fingers

some
vegetation

great
edges!

5.10c
fingers

5.9

5.8
thin hands

nuts

20' to
bolt

x

5.8R

5.7
hands

splitter crack

polished
edges

xx **B C D** 60'

set directional for follower

5.6

right easier

5.10d
move left

5.6

5.10a
dirty
awk. hands

5.10c

sustained
fingers/lieback

wavy crack
perfect hands

5.7
hands

5.10b
fingers

crystal
dish

micro
crack

5.8
polished
hands

5.10c
thin slab

xx **A** 45'

great
jams

5.10b
polished
fingers

5.8
lieback/jam

80 yards from hiker trail
300 yards from bridge

good hold
on left

3-4"

tricky 5.9
polished lieback

please stay on trail
to minimize erosion

Lost Arrow Spire

Chris McNamara

Located a few hundred yards from Upper Yosemite Fall, the Lost Arrow Spire is Yosemite's most striking pinnacle. The appeal lies in its fantastic form as well as the unique rope trick, a tyrolean traverse, required to escape the summit. Though reaching the tip requires only 250 feet of climbing, 1,500 feet of exposure gives this climb a distinct big wall feeling. This, combined with the gaping 80-foot gap between the spire and the wall, makes the Lost Arrow Spire possibly the most exhilarating two-pitch aid (or free) climb in Yosemite Valley.

Approach

There are two approaches: 1) From Camp 4, take the Yosemite Falls Trail. 3.6 miles of steep switchbacks lead to a trail junction. Walk east for 0.7 miles to Yosemite Point. From the railing, walk 100 yards west, along the rim, to a large tree that overlooks the Lost Arrow Spire. 2) A longer, but much flatter approach starts from the Porcupine Creek trailhead on Highway 120 and heads south, taking the shortest trail toward Yosemite Falls at each junction. (Do not take the Yosemite Creek Trail). The trail is a little over 5 miles long, is relatively flat, has some great views and takes two hours to reach the Spire. However, returning to your car involves long gradual uphill hiking at the end of the day.

Descent

Reverse the approach.

Lost Arrow Spire Tip

III 5.7 C2★★★★

Time to climb route:	**6 hours**
Approach time:	**3 hours**
Descent time:	**2 hours**
Sun exposure:	**morning to afternoon**
Height of route:	**250'**

Although it is only two pitches long, this route rewards you with one of the most spectacular settings in Yosemite. The climbing is technically easy and the gear is mostly fixed, but the long approach, big exposure and complex logistics make this route quite an undertaking. It is not recommended for a first aid climb.

History

The first ascents of the Lost Arrow Spire and the north face of Sentinel gave birth to the bold and committing style that inspired a radical change in big wall climbing. John Salathé not only revolutionized climbing hardware with his hard steel pitons on this route, he also dramatically raised the standard of technical difficulty.

Climbers had eyed the Spire for years but it wasn't until August 1946 that Salathé, alone, made the first attempt. After rappelling into the Notch behind the Arrow Tip, he discovered a line leading off a horrendously exposed ledge. Using a crude self-belay, Salathé nailed upward 20 feet to a blank spot. Here he placed the first bolt ever used on a climb for direct aid upward progress. After a second pitch he reached what today is known as Salathé Ledge before retreating back to the rim. Returning a week later with John Thune, Salathé pushed the route to within 30 feet of the

summit before the daunting expanse of blank rock stopped him cold.

In early September, after hearing of Salathé's near success on the Arrow Tip, a team of four climbers moved into action. Rather than finish the Salathé line, the team used what Steve Roper called "one of the greatest rope stunts ever pulled off in climbing history." From the rim the group took turns trying to throw the rope over the Arrow Tip to the opposite side. After a full day the perfect toss was made and the following day two of the four climbers, Ax Nelson and Jack Arnold, rappelled into the Notch and climbed up Salathé's route to Salathé Ledge. Here they picked up the end of the tossed line, which ran precariously over the tip and was then anchored to the rim. In classic mountaineering style, Ax Nelson had announced earlier on the climb, "The stern code of the climber decrees that the lightest man shall lead doubtful pitches." Arnold, being lighter than Nelson, smoked three cigarettes and then prusiked up the line to stand on the Spire's summit. Many climbers dismissed the ascent as a mere "rope trick," and not the least of the doubters was Salathé himself. Even Ax Nelson, who stood on the summit second after Arnold, realized that they hadn't really climbed the Tip.

That was to happen a year later, in September 1947, when Nelson teamed with Salathé to make the first true climbing ascent of the Lost Arrow Spire from the ground, using the byway of the Lost Arrow Chimney. A few parties had attempted this route but it was Salathé, with his hard steel pitons and relentless determination, who pushed to the summit. For the five-day climb the team brought a light rack of about 12 pitons, one lead rope, a couple of hauling ropes and only six quarts of water—an absurdly small amount. After five days of the most difficult climbing ever done on a long route, the pair stood on the summit. It was the world's first big wall aid climb and, perhaps, the most difficult rock climb in America and the world. This ascent gave birth to the Golden Age of Yosemite climbing. It inspired a new standard and changed climbing forever.

		Pitch	
Lost Arrow Spire		**1**	**2**
Aid Difficulty	A5/C5		
A = aid using hammer	A4/C4		
C = hammerless aid	A3/C3		
	A2/C2		
	A1/C1	**C**	**C**
Mandatory free	5.8-5.9		
	≤5.7	●	●

Dave Shultz et al made the first free ascent of the tip in 1984.

– *Chris McNamara*

Strategy

Most parties require more time than they anticipate. The route is popular—start early. This climb requires a tyrolean traverse (optional) and passing a knot while rappelling. Master these rope skills before the climb.

You need three ropes: one lead rope and two for rappelling into the notch.

Pitch 1 features startling exposure. At the top of the pitch is a 30-foot section of awkward 4" crack. If aiding, leapfrog large cams. If free climbing, push a large cam in front of you.

Pitch 2 is the crux and involves a few tricky placements and reaches. From the last bolt on the pitch, mandatory 5.5 friction climbing leads to the summit. Use many long slings on the pitch or these last 15 feet will have horrendous rope drag.

There are two options to get from the summit back to the rim. The easy way is to pull tight the ropes you trailed, attach your ascenders to the rope, set up a double-rope rappel off the spire and rap into the notch. The rope leading to the rim will come tight and you will begin moving away from the Spire toward the main wall. After rappelling 60 feet you will reach the wall and can jug up to the rim. A second way is with a tyrolean traverse, which is a good deal more complex but more classic (it is too lengthy and complex to describe here so consult a "How to Aid Climb" book.)

The ASCA has replaced most bolts. It is legal to camp 0.5 miles back from the Valley Rim and 100 yards away from any trail or water. The necessary wilderness permit can be obtained at the Wilderness Center but the quota often fills, so get your permit early the day before you climb.

Retreat

To retreat from below the spire's tip, rappel the climbing route back to The Notch and ascend your fixed rope back to the rim.

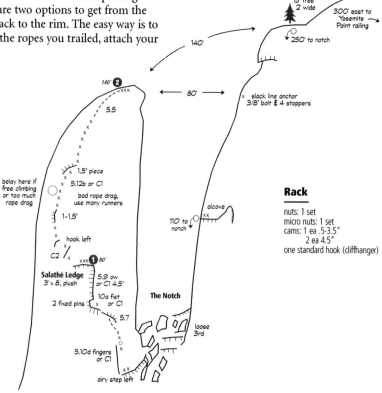

Rack

nuts: 1 set
micro nuts: 1 set
cams: 1 ea .5-3.5"
      2 ea 4.5"
one standard hook (cliffhanger)

Church Bowl

Approach time: 1 minute

Sun exposure: morning to afternoon

Height of routes: 175'

Church Bowl is the Valley's most accessible crag for full pitch moderate routes. The routes are great training with everything from chimneys to thin piton scars (for both aid and free climbing practice) to hand cracks. The routes have solid protection and are easy to retreat from. There are enough climbs for a full day of cragging.

Conditions in the spring and fall are perfect. In the summer, climb in the afternoon when the routes go into the shade.

Approach

Park 0.3 miles east of Yosemite Village, toward the Ahwahnee Hotel, at the Church Bowl picnic/parking area (a small brown sign can be seen beyond the trash cans). Walk 100 yards to the cliff.

Descent

Descend all routes by rappel; most require two ropes.

History

Climbers love short approaches, and the Church Bowl area just about wins any timed contest for car-to-cliff. The Church Bowl Chimney, a deep and nasty-looking cleft, was the first route to be done here, probably in the 1950s. Rated only 5.6, this strenuous route today stymies many gym climbers.

Next to fall was Bishop's Terrace. In late December 1959 I spied a beautiful set of jamcracks on the wall above and right of Church Bowl Chimney. Armed with the latest technology—heavy steel inch-and-a-half angle pitons—Dave McFadden, Russ Warne, and I swarmed up the easy lower section. But I didn't know squat about pure jamcracks, and I was scared to boot. To my everlasting shame I used two points of aid on the upper crack. Naturally, the route

Chris McNamara

1	Black is Brown	5	Book of Revelations
2	Uncle Fanny	6	Church Bowl Chimney
3	Church Bowl Lieback	7	Bishop's Terrace
4	Aunt Fanny's Pantry		

went free as soon as good climbers got on it, and this happened within months. Of course it was Chuck Pratt who led the first free ascent, so I didn't feel too bad.

Sheridan Anderson came along five years later to put up the pleasant Aunt Fanny's Pantry, with Leo LeBon. Sheridan was a true character, a mediocre climber with a love of beer and parties. His satirical climbing cartoons, mostly published in Summit, delighted us for a decade.

Next came the longest route in this area, Book of Revelations, put up in 1965 by Gordie Webster and Chuck Ostin. This pair used a fair amount of aid on their five-pitch line, but the route was freed at 11a (with the help of old pin scars) nine years later.

– Steve Roper

A. Black is Brown   5.8★★

FA: Kim Schmitz and Frank Trummel, 1966.

A moderate quality steep crack. Rappel to descend. You can also descend 4th class to the left (west).

B. Deja Thorus   5.10a★

FA: Jim Beyer and Misa Giesey, 1978.

This route involves sustained liebacking with a few face moves. It is not a popular lead, but a fun toprope from the Uncle

Fanny belay anchors. Multiple directionals must be set down the flake for toproping, since a nasty fall into the corner could otherwise result.

C. Uncle Fanny   5.7★★

FA: Bruce Price and Michael McLean, 1/70.

A good introduction to chimney climbing. Low angle chimney has excellent 1-2" gear in back. Above, put left side of body into the crack and use heel/toe technique.

D. Church Bowl Lieback   5.8★★★★

This is one of the best climbs at the crag. Use many long slings and take the left finish. This is a good lead to set topropes on other nearby climbs. To belay for a toprope, scramble up to the ledge 10 feet above the ground.

E. Pole Position   5.10a★★

FA: John Harpole et al, late 1980s.

A good introductory friction climb that is unfortunately situated with a nasty fall for the leader (or follower) onto a tree after the second bolt. Excellent climbing on knobs and edges higher. Use directionals on the bolts if toproping.

F. Revival   5.10a★★

Great crack climbing followed by face moves. Use many long slings to avoid rope drag. If toproping, climb straight up from the ground on either side of a large block.

G. Aunt Fanny's Pantry   5.4★

FA: Sheridan Anderson and Leo LeBon, 1965.

This easy and unaesthetic chimney is a good entry-level climb and can be used to access toprope anchors.

H. Book of Revelations (first two pitches) 5.11a★★★★

FA: Gordon Webster, Chuck Ostin, 10/65.
FFA: Bob Finn, Chris Falkenstein, 1974.

An extremely awkward crux after 20 feet is followed by hard moves and awkward rests. The crux is often wet during early season and the upper pitches (not shown) are rarely climbed.

I. Church Bowl Tree   5.10b★★★

FA: Mark Jefferson and Dave Collins, 8/70.

Great training for free climbing or hammerless aid on pin scars. The route involves finger jams in scars and balancy mantels. Getting off the ground can be tricky due to the polish. Most climbers only do the first pitch.

J. Church Bowl Chimney   5.6★★

The next step in chimney training after Uncle Fanny. Great route for doing laps and practicing steep stemming.

K. Energizer   5.11b★★★

FA: Dan and Sue McDevitt, 1990.

Well-protected with bolts, this is a great climb to get comfortable on steep Yosemite face climbing. Crux moves consist of smears and delicate balancy moves to small edges.

L. Bitches' Terror   5.11a★★★

FA: Walt Shipley and Eric Kohl, 1990.

A quality steep face climb. Approach via the first short pitch of Bishop's Terrace, or better yet, warm up on Bishop's Terrace then rappel 80 feet down and left to the bolt anchor at the start.

M. Bishop's Terrace   5.8★★★★★

FA: Russ Warne, Dave McFadden, and Steve Roper, 12/59.
FFA: Chuck Pratt and Herb Swedlund, 1960.

One of the best 5.8 hand cracks in the Valley. Of the two starts, the left one is recommended. Climb in two pitches with 50m ropes or in one pitch with a 60m rope and use many slings down low. The climbing consists of glorious hand jams, a brief wide section, and double cracks. If using the alternate right start, it is possible to climb to the upper anchors with one 50m rope. You need a second rope to rappel to the ground.

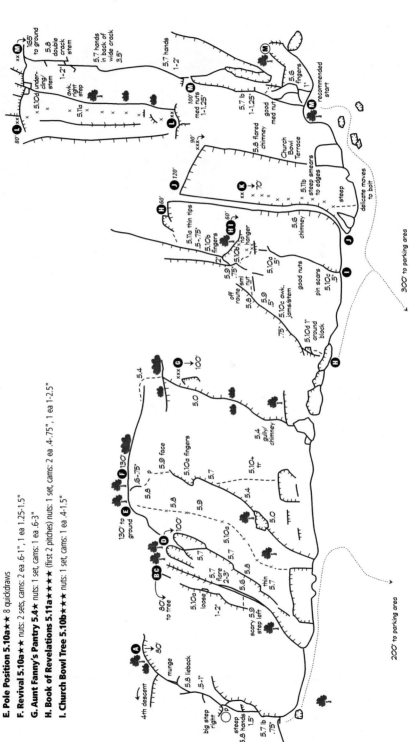

A. Black is Brown 5.8★★ nuts: 1 set, cams: 2 ea .5-1.5"

B. Deja Thorus 5.10a★ nuts: 1 set, cams: 2 ea .6-3"

C. Uncle Fanny 5.7★★ nuts: 1 set, cams: 1 ea .6-.75", 2 ea 1-2", 1 ea 3"

D. Church Bowl Lieback 5.8★★★★★ nuts: 1 set

E. Pole Position 5.10a★★ 8 quickdraws

F. Revival 5.10a★★ nuts: 2 sets, cams: 2 ea .6-1", 1 ea 1.25-1.5"

G. Aunt Fanny's Pantry 5.4★ nuts: 1 set, cams: 1 ea .6-3"

H. Book of Revelations 5.11a★★★★ (first 2 pitches) nuts: 1 set, cams: 2 ea .4-.75", 1 ea 1-2.5"

I. Church Bowl Tree 5.10b★★★ nuts: 1 set, cams: 1 ea .4-1.5"

J. Church Bowl Chimney 5.6★★ nuts: 1 set, cams: 1 ea 1-3.5"

K. Energizer 5.11b★★★ 10 quickdraws

L. Bitches' Terror 5.11a★★ 10 quickdraws

M. Bishop's Terrace 5.8★★★★★ nuts: 1 set, cams: 1 ea 1-3.5", 2 ea 1-2.5", 1 ea 3.5"

North Dome Gully

The North Dome Gully requires tricky routefinding on exposed terrain. It is strongly advised that you travel with someone who is familiar with the descent. If it is your first time and you must descend at night or in a storm, consider hiking to the North Dome Trail and walking about 8 miles to Camp 4.

Mark Kroese

From Royal Arches Last Pitch

If you have the North Dome Gully memorized, it is the fastest way to descend from Royal Arches and takes 1-2 hours. If it is not familiar, the North Dome Gully can be a nightmare and take 4 hours due to the ease of getting off route. We strongly recommended the Royal Arches Rappel Route (a topo is located with the SuperTopo for the Royal Arches route).

From the last pitch of Royal Arches, follow a climbers' trail west (some 3rd and 4th class required) to the **rim (1)**. Continue on the climbers' trail as it turns east. For the next 5-10 minutes the trail will stay roughly 100-300 feet north of the edge. The trail eventually moves north (farther from the edge) and enters bushy terrain, then **trees (2)**. The climbers' trail leaves the trees and continues through manzanita as it climbs up to a **ridge (3)**. Next, follow the instructions in the section titled, "From Washington Column Ridge."

From Washington Column Summit

This is the best descent option for Washington Column and takes 1-3 hours.

From the top of Washington Column, walk north toward North Dome on a climbers' trail through manzanita staying just west and below the ridge. After 5-10 minutes gain the **ridge (3)**. Next, follow the instructions in the section titled, "From Washington Column Ridge."

From Washington Column Ridge

From the ridge, walk north, and look for a sandy, mildly exposed **climbers' trail (4)** that drops down the east side of the ridge and then continues traversing exposed terrain. This trail is difficult to locate but once you find it, the climbers' trail is well-defined. The next 100 yards are the crux. In general, traverse horizontally without ever gaining or losing more than 100 feet of elevation. If you ever contemplate a steep rap, you are off route.

A few hundred feet after leaving the ridge, work briefly up an **eroding hillside (5)** then move down and make a short but exposed **4th class traverse (6)**. Move back up a short section and then continue traversing above an **exposed cliff (7)** until it is mandatory to downclimb 40 feet of **4th class and tree branches (8)**. From here, move east, cross a 50-foot-wide rocky **drainage (9)**, and continue traversing east into the trees until a steep, slippery, and dusty trail leads down through the **trees (10)**. This trail leads out into the open to a long section of loose but well-worn **switchbacks (11)**. These switchbacks lead to a few short but exposed sections of **4th class down climbing (12)** that some parties may want to rappel (there are bolts but sometimes no slings.) From the base of the North Dome Gully, either skirt the base back to the east face of Washington Column or continue straight down on a well-worn **climbers' trail (13)** that eventually leads to the horse trail and then the **bike path (14)** near the Indian Caves. Follow the bike path or horse trail back to the **Ahwahnee Hotel (15)**.

North Dome

to Tuolumne

South Face

Chris McNamara

North Dome is a Tuolumne-like dome with Yosemite Valley quality rock. One of Yosemite's larger domes, most ignore it due to a long approach and little publicity. Those willing to hike will find great climbing with stunning views of Yosemite Valley.

Approach

North Dome can be accessed via a trail from Tamarack Flat or by climbing the Royal Arches route or a Washington Column route. The recommended approach is to climb Royal Arches.

From the top of Royal Arches, head east along the descent trail until reaching the slabs that lead toward North Dome. Walk up and slightly right over the slabs aiming for the lower of the two obvious terraces with trees at the base of North Dome. Skirt a large rock ridge along its left side and gain the base of the dome at the eastern end of the terrace. The route begins at the obvious huge left-facing dihedral.

Descent

From the top of the route, head up and left toward the summit of North Dome. Once on the summit, descend the north side to the trees. A trail through the trees leads down and west along the base of the dome. Follow this trail down and around the dome until reaching the same slabs used for the approach. Head down these slabs to the trail that leads across (east) and over Washington Column. Descend to the valley via the North Dome Gully. A SuperTopo is available and strongly recommended for the North Dome Gully descent.

South Face

III 5.8★★★★

Time to climb route: **5.5-6 hours**

Approach time: **1-6 hours**

Descent time: **2-3 hours**

Sun exposure: **morning to afternoon**

Height of route: **950'**

The South Face route follows an obvious dihedral and crack system up one of Yosemite Valley's true domes. The route requires every technique, especially liebacking. Every pitch is fun, but it is the wild, low traverse and incredible liebacking up high that make this climb memorable. The arduous approach and descent make for a long day, but are worth the effort.

History

Wally Reed and Mark Powell were the two best Valley free climbers during the late 1950s. Much of the time they climbed with others, but during the spring and summer of 1957 they got together and established five exceptional routes. Among these is one of the classics of today, the South Face of North Dome.

Distinguished by its remoteness, its ultra-clean rock, its moderate climbing, and its stunning view of the face of Half Dome, the route is a true gem. There's only one problem: the approach. If the route were down near the Valley floor it would be climbed as often as the Nutcracker. As it is, it's a neglected beauty.

Reed described the climb later in his matter-of-fact style. "After three pitches of easy friction and lieback climbing we were at the base of a 15-foot overhanging wall which diagonals to the left across the lower third of the face. Three sixth-class pitons overcame that problem, which was followed by two moderate friction pitches." Soon the pair arrived at the crux, a right-facing open book that stretched upward out of sight. Reed again: "Arranging a belay stance from a lieback position 100 feet up was difficult, as was the single crack which continued to a small ledge above and which was partly filled with dirt and grass. Thirty feet beyond the ledge all cracks terminated. By placing a piton at his feet, Mark was able to make a difficult pull-up and a delicate friction step to easy scrambling and the summit. It took us about six hours."

Reed and Powell had accomplished the route in superb style, using only three aid placements. Other climbers of the time would have used many more.

Because of the gruesome approach, no one repeated this route for more than three years. One cool October morning in 1960, I was restless, eager to do something different from the usual routine. I talked Mort Hempel and Irene Ortenburger into trying the route, and soon we were staggering up the North Dome Gully, complaining just as much as Reed and Powell must have done. But, unlike them, we still had the climb ahead of us on the same day, and didn't rope up until early afternoon. We somehow avoided the aid on the "15-foot overhanging wall" (it seemed not that overhung and only wild 5.7, so perhaps we discovered a variation), and then raced the sun to the top. The liebacks at the top proved thrilling indeed, but the descent was not. In fading light and then starlight we followed the 8-mile trail back to Camp 4, arriving at 10 p.m. A long day!

– *Steve Roper*

South Face		Pitch 1	2	3	4	5	6	7
Free difficulty	≥5.10							
	5.9							
	5.8							
	5.7			●	●	●		
	5.6	●	●				●	●
	≤5.5							

Strategy

The route begins above the Valley rim so an
early start is required. A 60m rope allows
linking some pitches and is needed to avoid
simul-climbing on Pitch 4 (180 feet).

The crux of Pitch 3 is negotiating the
odd sequence of ledges to move from the
dihedral to the crack on the right face.
Climb up the dihedral to ledges on the right
(well below the first of two sets of off-route
slings). Protect in a flake and climb up and
right onto a higher ledge, then move back
down onto the lower ledge. Yet another
ledge heads around the corner—move onto
that large ledge via an awkward move (note
the hole in the ledge for a good handhold!)
and continue around right. A few face
moves right gains the crack, which is
climbed to the belay.

The South Face of North Dome receives
sun all day and can be warm in the
summer. The route can also be cold and
windy during any season—prepare for any
weather conditions that may develop
during the day. North Dome is struck by
lightning quite often during storms. Review
weather forecasts and learn proper
techniques for extreme conditions.

Retreat

Rap slings from trees facilitate retreat from
Pitch 1 or 2. Beyond Pitch 2, retreat would
be possible, but would require leaving gear.
Either of these retreat options will require
two 50m ropes.

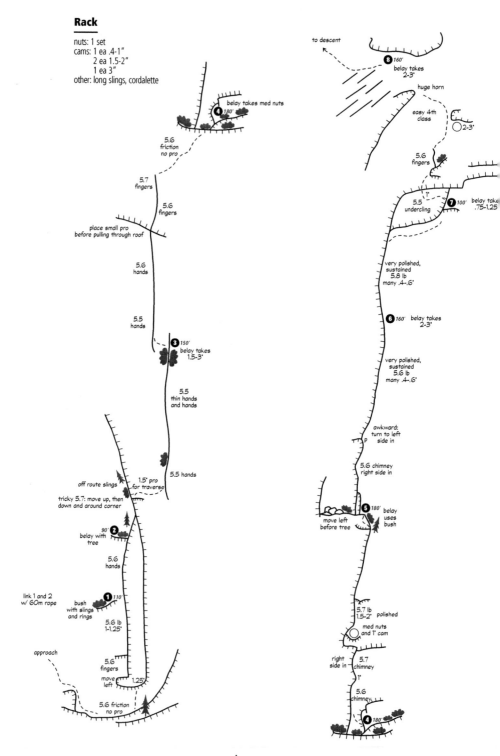

Rack

nuts: 1 set
cams: 1 ea .4-1"
2 ea 1.5-2"
1 ea 3"
other: long slings, cordalette

belay takes med nuts

4 180'

5.6
friction
no pro

5.7
fingers

5.6
fingers

place small pro
before pulling through roof

5.6
hands

5.5
hands

3 150' belay takes
1.5-3'

5.5
thin hands
and hands

5.5 hands

off route slings

1.5' pro
for traverse

tricky 5.7: move up, then
down and around corner

2 90'
belay with
tree

5.6
hands

link 1 and 2
w/ 60m rope

1 110'
bush
with slings
and rings

5.6 lb
1-1.25'

approach

5.6
fingers

move
left

1.25'

5.6 friction
no pro

to descent

8 160'
belay takes
2-3'

huge horn

easy 4th
class

2-3'

5.6
fingers

1"

5.5
undercling

7 100' belay take
.75-1.25

very polished,
sustained
5.8 lb
many .4-.6'

6 160' belay takes
2-3'

very polished,
sustained
5.6 lb
many .4-.6'

awkward:
turn to left
side in

5.6 chimney
right side in

5 180' belay
uses
bush

move left
before tree

5.7 lb
1.5-2' polished

med nuts
and 1' cam

right
side in

5.7
chimney

1'

5.6
chimney

4 180'

Half Dome, Northwest Face

Mark Kroese

Under the face of Half Dome is one of the most impressive spots on earth. El Capitan is higher; the Cathedral Spires are more like towers. But the awe of a single sheet of granite tapestry almost half a mile high and half a mile wide is unparalleled. The ascent of this face in 1957 put Yosemite on the mountaineering map. For the first time, climbers in Europe realized that Americans were developing a separate and at least equal brand of rock climbing.

– *Galen Rowell,* The Vertical World of Yosemite, 1974

Approach

There are two ways to approach the Northwest Face of Half Dome: the Half Dome Trail and "The Slabs." Hiking the John Muir Trail to the Half Dome Trail from Happy Isles to the eastern shoulder of Half Dome (7.5 miles, 4-6 hours) and then following a climbers' trail to the base (0.5 mile, 20 minutes) is the straightforward, but grueling option. "The Slabs," although technically more difficult, is much faster and can mean the difference between being first or fifth in line for the Regular Northwest Face. For either approach park at Curry Village.

The Slabs Approach

This approach requires 2-4 hours. From Curry Village, take the bus to the stop for Mirror Lake. Walk on the road to Tenaya Bridge. From here follow "The Slabs Approach" topo.

Descending The Slabs

Descend The Slabs only if retreating from the base of the Northwest Face (from the summit, it is much better to descend via the Half Dome Trail.)

To descend The Slabs, either descend the way you approached, or before entering the main drainage (under "mouth of drainage" on topo), continue down the trail (west of drainage) until reaching the edge of a cliff above the drainage and a tree with rap slings. A 50m rap brings you back to the regular approach descent route.

Descending the Half Dome Trail

This descent requires 3-5 hours and is the recommended way to descend from the summit. Starting from the cables, follow the Half Dome Trail 2.6 miles to the John Muir Trail. Follow the Muir Trail for 6.5 miles to Happy Isles and the Valley floor. From Happy Isles, take the bus back to Curry Village or walk the road.

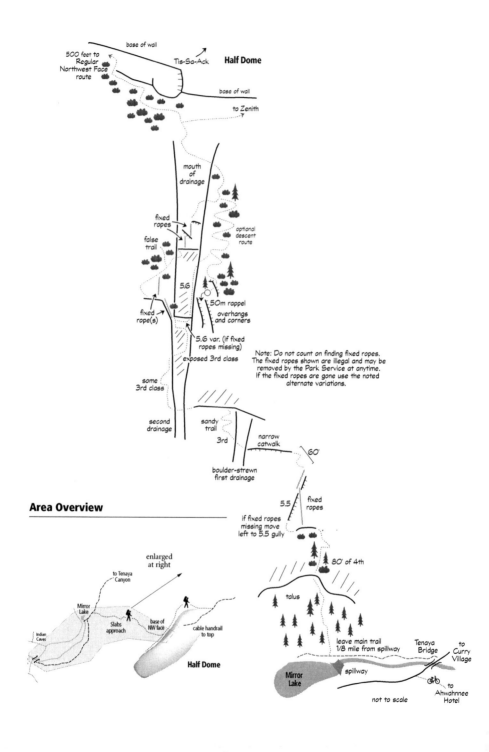

base of wall

500 feet to
Regular
Northwest Face
route

Tis-Sa-Ack   **Half Dome**

base of wall

to Zenith

mouth
of
drainage

fixed
ropes

optional
descent
route

false
trail

5.6

50m rappel

fixed
rope(s)

overhangs
and corners

5.6 var. (if fixed
ropes missing)

exposed 3rd class

Note: Do not count on finding fixed ropes.
The fixed ropes shown are illegal and may be
removed by the Park Service at anytime.
If the fixed ropes are gone use the noted
alternate variations.

some
3rd class

second
drainage

sandy
trail

3rd

narrow
catwalk

60'

boulder-strewn
first drainage

5.5

fixed
ropes

if fixed ropes
missing move
left to 5.5 gully

Area Overview

80' of 4th

enlarged
at right

to Tenaya
Canyon

talus

Mirror
Lake

Slabs
approach

base of
NW face

cable handrail
to top

Indian
Caves

leave main trail
1/8 mile from spillway

Tenaya
Bridge

to
Curry
Village

Half Dome

Mirror
Lake

spillway

to
Ahwahnee
Hotel

not to scale

Regular Northwest Face

VI 5.12 or 5.8 C1★★★★★

Time to climb route:	**3 days**
Approach time:	**3 hours**
Descent time:	**4 hours**
Sun exposure:	**afternoon to sunset**
Height of route:	**2000'**

The long approach and north-facing orientation give the Regular Northwest Face an alpine quality not found on other Yosemite walls. The climbing starts off wandering at a low angle and gradually grows steeper. The last seven pitches are spectacular. Place one South Face of the Column on top of another and you will get an idea of the Regular Northwest Face's length and difficulty.

History

The first day, Royal Robbins, Mike Sherrick, and Jerry Gallwas climbed the broken, lower-angle initial pitches until faced with a seemingly blank expanse of granite. Robbins overcame this section by placing seven bolts and then making the most audacious pendulum yet completed in Yosemite on what was later named the Robbins Traverse.

Above, the team found heads-up climbing through loose chockstone-choked chimneys. Two committing features, the Undercling Flake and Psych Flake, were especially unnerving and with good reason—years later they both fell off! The fourth day presented the crux Zig Zags. Two hundred feet of difficult nailing up elegant and steep corners brought the tired climbers to a claustrophobic alcove for their fourth and last bivy. Adding to their

discomfort that evening was the Visor, an enormous tiered roof that loomed above, possibly blocking passage to the summit.

To their great relief a sliver of perfect granite dubbed Thank God Ledge materialized the next day, leading the climbers under the Visor to easier ground. On June 28, 1957, the evening of their fifth day, Robbins, Gallwas, and Sherrick stood on the summit, having completed the most difficult wall in North America.

In 1975, Jim Erickson and Art Higbee freed all but a short section of the route (above Thank God Ledge) at 5.12b. Erickson returned later and freed this section on toprope.

– Chris McNamara

Strategy

The key to enjoying this route is to move light and fast and bivy only once. If you take longer prepare yourself for bad hauling and bivy ledges. Fast teams spend day one approaching the wall and fixing to Pitch 3, day two climbing to Big Sandy Ledge, and day three topping out. Slower parties spend two nights on the wall and endure an uncomfortable bivy at 6 or 11 and then Big Sandy. In summer, two to five parties often converge at the base so approach early and plan on a day waiting in line. The moves are technically easy at 5.8 C1, but a 5.10 leader will have increased odds of success and better enjoy the climb.

Retreat

Half Dome is more susceptible to poor weather than most Valley big walls. Thunderstorms can hit the face with rain, hail, wind, and lightning. Retreat at any point by rappelling the route.

Regular NW Face		Pitch 1	2	3	4	5	6	7	8	9	10	11	12	13	14	15	16	17	18	19	20	21	22	23
Aid	A5/C5																							
A = aid using hammer	A4/C4																							
C = hammerless aid	A3/C3																							
	A2/C2																							
	A1/C1	C	C	C	C	C	C	C	C			C	C	C		C	C	C	C	C	C		C	C
Mandatory free	5.8-5.9													●							●			
	≤5.7		●	●			●			●			●	●	●									

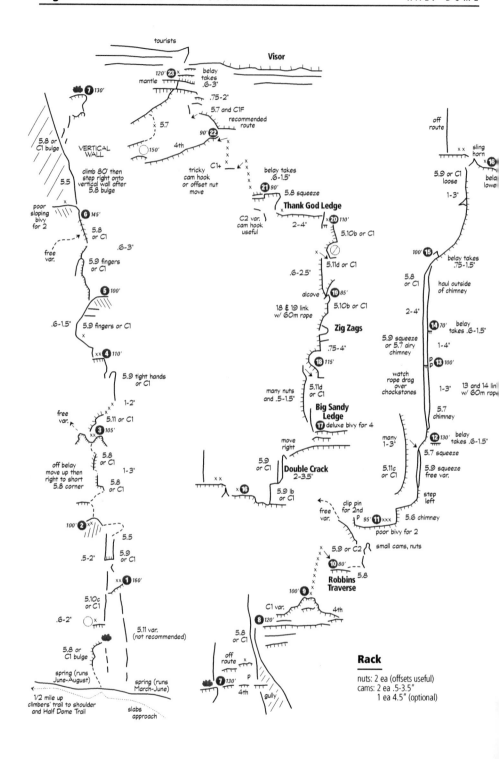

tourists

Visor

120' 23 x
mantle
belay
takes
.6-3"

.75-2"

5.7 and C1F
recommended
route

7 130'

x 5.7

90' 22

off
route

5.8 or
C1 bulge

VERTICAL
WALL

150' 4th

x x sling
horn

x x

16

5.5

climb 80' then
step right onto
vertical wall after
5.8 bulge

tricky
cam hook
or offset nut
move

C1+ x
x
x
x
x

belay takes
.6-1.5"

5.9 or C1
loose

1-3"

bela
lowe

21 90'

5.8 squeeze

poor
sloping
bivy
for 2

x
6 145'

Thank God Ledge

5.8
or C1

.6-3"

C2 var.
cam hook
useful

2-4"

x 20 110'

5.10b or C1

100' 15

belay takes
.75-1.5"

free
var.

5.9 fingers
or C1

x

5.11d or C1

5.8
or C1

haul outside
of chimney

5 100'

.6-2.5"

2-4"

.6-1.5"

5.9 fingers or C1

alcove

19 85'

5.10b or C1

14 70'

belay
takes .6-1.5"

x

x x 4 110'

18 & 19 link
w/ 60m rope

1-4"

Zig Zags

5.9 squeeze
or 5.7 airy
chimney

5.9 tight hands
or C1

18 115'

watch
rope drag
over
chockstones

1-3"

P
P 13 100'

1-2"

many nuts
and .5-1.5"

5.11d
or C1

13 and 14 lin
w/ 60m rope

free
var.

x x x x
3 105'

5.11 or C1

xx

**Big Sandy
Ledge**

5.7
chimney

17 deluxe bivy for 4

many
1-3"

12 130'

belay
takes .6-1.5"

5.7 squeeze

off belay
move up then
right to short
5.8 corner

5.8
or C1

1-3"

move
right

5.11c
or C1

5.9 squeeze
free var.

5.8
or C1

5.9
or C1

Double Crack
2-3.5"

step
left

100' 2 xx

5.5

x x

5.6 chimney

.5-2"

5.9
or C1

x 16

5.9 lb
or C1

free
var.

clip pin
for 2nd

P 95' 11 xxx

poor bivy for 2

xx 1 160'

5.9 or C2

small cams, nuts

x
x
x
10 80'

5.10c
or C1

5.11 var.
(not recommended)

100' 9

x
x
x
x
x
x

5.8

**Robbins
Traverse**

.6-2"

x

C1 var.

4th

5.8 or
C1 bulge

8 120'

spring (runs
June-August)

spring (runs
March-June)

5.8
or C1

off
route x
x

1/2 mile up
climbers' trail to shoulder
and Half Dome Trail

slabs
approach

7 130'
4th

P

gully

Rack

nuts: 2 ea (offsets useful)
cams: 2 ea .5-3.5"
1 ea 4.5" (optional)

Half Dome, Southwest Face

Snake Dike

Chris McNamara

In his book *The Yosemite*, John Muir called Half Dome, "the most beautiful and sublime of all the wonderful Yosemite rocks." With a summit that towers nearly 5,000 feet above the Yosemite Valley floor and a sheer face of 2,000 vertical feet, Half Dome offers breathtaking views of Yosemite Valley and the High Sierra.

In the 1860s, the California Geological Survey deemed Half Dome unclimbable, "a perfectly inaccessible [peak] which never has been, and never will be, trodden by human foot." But in 1875, George Anderson, a Scottish trail-builder and carpenter made it to the summit. He painstakingly drilled 6-inch-deep holes into the 300-foot 45-degree eastern slab. After hammering iron pegs into these holes, Anderson was able to attach ropes and ascend the dome. Just days later, Sandy Dutcher, wearing a long dress, became the first woman to climb Half Dome.

Approach

The 6-mile approach is extremely strenuous. Start early and plan for at least 3 hours of hiking. Park either at Curry Village or the Stables (no overnight parking) and walk or take the shuttle bus to Happy Isles. Follow the John Muir Trail for 1 mile to the Mist Trail. Follow the Mist Trail for 2.1 miles to the top of Nevada Fall and again pick up the Muir Trail. After about 0.75 miles, the rock on the left that forms the shoulder of Liberty Cap will gradually recede to nothing. At this point, pick up a climbers' trail on the left and walk northwest for about 1 mile, passing Lost Lake, to the open slabs. Here the trail ends and you must walk directly toward the South Face of Half Dome on talus and slabs with some bushwhacking. Cairns are abundant and may or may not guide you on the right path. Skirt the base of the south face on sometimes exposed ledges and 3rd and 4th class to the sandy switchbacks that lead to the base of the Southwest Face and the start of the route.

Approach between Mt. Broderick and Liberty Cap: This more scenic variation is slightly faster but devious. Few people find the fastest way on their first attempt. On the Mist Trail, before the final steep granite switchbacks leading to the top of Nevada Fall, pick up a climbers' trail to the left when Liberty Cap touches the trail. Skirt the base of the South Face of Liberty Cap. Follow cairns and switchbacks up and right through the trees to an open talus slope that leads to the base of a steep cliff. Contour left along the cliff, following it as it trends right above a steep drop-off and drops down slightly left into the chasm between Mt. Broderick and Liberty Cap. Continue through the chasm (stay right) and scramble up 3rd class rocks as the brush becomes thicker. Near the top of the chasm, move left into a flat area and follow a streambed. Trend back right and into trees until Half Dome becomes visible on the left—at this point look for cairns leading left. Follow the trail north, then east and merge with the standard approach at Lost Lake.

Descent

Allow 3-4 hours for the 9-mile descent. From the summit, descend the cables. The cables are in place year-round. During the winter and spring uprights are removed, but the cables are still easy to descend. Continue on the Half Dome Trail until it joins the Muir Trail, which leads back to Happy Isles.

Snake Dike

III 5.7 R★★★★★

Time to climb route: **3-4 hours**

Approach time: **3-4 hours**

Descent time: **3-4 hours**

Sun exposure: **late morning to sunset**

Height of route: **800'**

Snake Dike is the easiest technical climbing route to the top of Half Dome, the most striking rock feature in the United States. The unreal summit rises 5,000 feet above the Yosemite Valley floor and offers amazing views of Yosemite and the High Sierra. This dramatic setting, along with clean and exposed climbing, make Snake Dike one of the most glorious moderate climbs on the planet. The long and aesthetic approach will take you past two beautiful waterfalls, through the backcountry and past an isolated lake to the southwest toe of Half Dome. The route climbs an 800-foot salmon-colored dike that wanders up the dramatic southwest face of Half Dome. The combination of a 6-mile hike to the base, eight pitches of climbing, and a 9-mile descent back to the Valley makes for a full adventure and may require more than one day.

History

Climbers who made the long trek up to the base of the massive southwest face of Half Dome before 1965 went there for one reason only: to do the classic Salathé-Nelson route. This demanding aid line wandered up unconnected crack systems, but it was the only way to the top: everyone knew that the rest of the wide face was crackless—obviously impossible. When

Camp 4 inhabitants heard, in July 1965, that a second route had been put up nearby, the sense of disbelief was audible. When the first ascensionists—Eric Beck, Jim Bridwell, and Chris Fredericks—bragged that their route was trivial, disbelief turned to disdain. When they claimed that they had placed only two pitons and about six hurried bolts, disdain evolved to thoughts that the three men should be committed. A far easier route than Salathé's? But it was true. Beck had been the instigator of the route soon named Snake Dike; he had spotted a potential route on a reconnaissance and had talked the two others into making the horrendous approach. To their great surprise they put up the new route in a day from Camp 4 back to Camp 4.

Years later, Beck reminisced about their climb. "We were expecting a much harder route and only had twelve bolts, so we did our best to conserve them where the climbing was easy. What I really imagined happening was that we would get up a few pitches, fix the ropes, and return with more bolts. Also, our original choice of line was to follow a dike leading up and right, on pitch three. This was Bridwell's lead and he climbed up about 20 feet, got in a bolt, but didn't like it. This caused more uncertainty about routefinding and wasting our bolts. I then gained the lead and had a look to the left. This proved to be the best way."

Two years later I grabbed a stranger named John Gibbons and we set off at dawn from a campsite in Little Yosemite, armed with a hefty bolt kit. Ordinarily, taking a bolt kit for an easy second ascent would have made me a laughingstock. But Beck, Bridwell, and Fredericks, feeling that they had created a potential death route for beginners, had given me permission to replace their bad bolts and stick in new ones where I deemed necessary. This was the first time in Valley history that first ascensionists had given someone permission to add bolts to their route.

At the end of two pitches Gibbons and I realized that the Dike was truly a splendid route, and I made sure my bolts were bombproof and properly spaced. That is, I

Snake Dike		Pitch							
		1	2	3	4	5	6	7	8
Free difficulty	≥5.10								
	5.9								
	5.8								
	5.7	●	●	●					
	5.6				●				
	≤5.5					●		●	● ●

did this for a while. My fingers and arms soon began to throb from all the hand drilling. Morning turned to afternoon. I inspected my dulled drill bits. I listened as Gibbons called up anxiously, "You finished?" Soon I simply ran out the pitches and relied on the sporadic and wretched first ascent bolts. We rappelled the route and staggered down through the brush to our camp below, arriving just as the owls began to hoot.

Snake Dike hadn't been totally retrofitted, but it had been a good day and a good start. We spread the word and within a few years many bolts were added, and Snake Dike became the most popular climbers' route to the top of the most spectacular hunk of granite in North America.

– Steve Roper

Mark Kroese

Strategy

Start early, as the day will be long. Snake Dike is a popular route so be prepared for a wait at the base, unexpected weather changes, and a late finish. A 60m rope allows more options of linking pitches, but is not required. Many of the belays are at small stances, so comfortable climbing shoes are recommended.

The first pitch crux offers the option climbing high up and right to set pro then back down before moving left to 5.7 friction. The third pitch crux is both the technical and psychological crux of the climb: an exposed 5.7 friction traverse. At the end of the traverse is an alternate belay/rap station with two bolts. To better protect your follower on the traverse, clip these bolts with an extra long sling or skip the bolts and climb up the dike to the next bolt which offers a better rope angle for the follower on the friction traverse. From here on up, easier grade climbing wanders up the salmon-colored dike for four pitches with very runout 5.4 R and 5.3 R sections. On the typical runout pitch, you will climb as much as 75 feet of 5.4 R without any protection, clip a bolt, and then climb another 75 feet of 5.4 R to the anchor. Careful climbing is warranted on these

dangerously runout sections, but the climbing is amazing, with numerous bomber jugs.

The sun hits the climb by mid-morning and temperatures range from very hot to windy and cold. During the summer, afternoon thunderstorms are common and lightning strikes on Half Dome's summit have resulted in death. Be aware of approaching thunderclouds and do not hesitate to retreat if the risk of lightning arises.

Many climbers give themselves more time by camping at either Lost Lake or Little Yosemite Valley the night before starting the route. Consult the Wilderness Center for permits and information or visit www.nps.gov/yose/wilderness/permits.htm.

Wild-at-heart climbers are sometimes found climbing this route by full moon.

Retreat

The route can be rappelled easily from any point using two 50m ropes.

More at SuperTopo.com

Get a free color download of this topo at: www.supertopo.com/freetopos.html

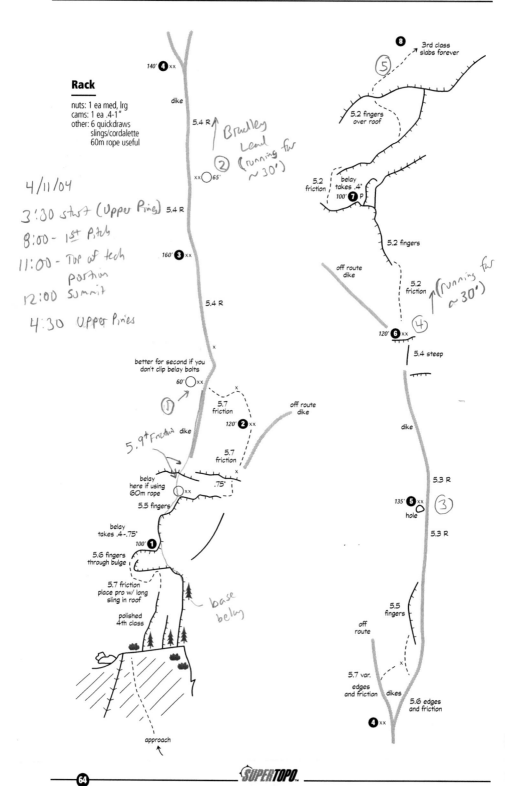

Rack

nuts: 1 ea med, lrg
cams: 1 ea .4-1"
other: 6 quickdraws
    slings/cordalette
    60m rope useful

4/11/04

3:30 start (Upper Pines)

8:00 - 1st Pitch

11:00 - Top of tech
    portion

12:00 Summit

4:30 Upper Pines

140' **4** xx

dike

5.4 R

Bradley
Lead
(running for
~30')

2 65'
xx xx

5.4 R

160' **3** xx

5.4 R

x

better for second if you
don't clip belay bolts

60' xx

(1)

5.9+ Friction dike

5.7
friction

120' **2** xx

off route
dike

5.7
friction

belay
here if using
60m rope xx

.75"
x

x

5.5 fingers

belay
takes .4-.75'

100' **1**

5.6 fingers
through bulge

5.7 friction
place pro w/ long
sling in roof

base
belay

polished
4th class

approach

8

3rd class
slabs forever

(5)

5.2 fingers
over roof

5.2
friction

belay
takes .4"
100' **7** P

5.2 fingers

off route
dike

5.2
friction

(running for
~30')

120' **6** xx

(4)

5.4 steep

dike

5.3 R

135' **5** xx
hole

(3)

5.3 R

5.5
fingers

off
route

x

5.7 var.
edges
and friction   dikes

5.6 edges
and friction

4 xx

Higher Cathedral Spire

Higher Cathedral Spire was considered the "testpiece" Valley climb at the time of the first ascent in 1934 by climbing legends, Jules Eichorn, Bestor Robinson, and Dick Leonard. During the 1930s the techniques for roped climbing were still new and the modern climber can only imagine the terror of climbing this classic route wearing heavy boots, almost no pro for the leader, and ropes that were unlikely to survive a lead fall.

Approach

The approach to Higher Cathedral Spire is started from one of two parking areas along Southside Drive, 100 yards before the Highway 120/140/41 cutoff. If coming from the Valley, turn left before El Cap Meadow and park on the left at the merge. Walk back along the road to the paved pullout on the south side of the road.

From this pullout, hike into the trees past the carabiner post and intersect the main trail running east/west. Head east (left) and hike 0.25 mile to a distinct trail heading south into the trees marked by two large downed trees. This trail is not marked by a carabiner post. Follow this trail up switchbacks to the talus slope. Cairns mark the easiest path up the talus. Trend left whenever there is any question. Continue past the Lower Cathedral Spire and follow the contour of the west face of Higher Cathedral Spire up and around the south side. The trail is well-traveled and switchbacks up loose dirt and talus, then cuts left to a cleft at the start of the route. A cross is etched into the rock at the base of the route.

Regular Route

Greg Barnes

Descent

Rappel the route and reverse the approach. You can rappel the route with one 50m rope, but it is much easier with a 60m rope.

Regular Route

III 5.9★★★★★

Time to climb route:	**3-4 hours**
Approach time:	**1.5-2 hours**
Descent time:	**1 hour rappel and 1.5 hours to car**
Sun exposure:	**noon to afternoon**
Height of route:	**300'**

To stand on the exceptional summit of Higher Cathedral Spire, North America's highest free-standing pinnacle is truly an experience. The route was first climbed in 1934 and was made with antiquated climbing equipment. The featured rock has wild face moves so rare in Yosemite where most faces are polished and featureless.

History

It's hardly surprising that the pioneer climbers of the early 1930s chose the Higher Cathedral Spire for their first serious outing. These adventurers had started as mountaineers, where reaching an actual summit (rather than a nondescript rim or a ledge partway up a cliff) was a demonstrable sign of success. And what better place to head for than the Higher Spire, North America's largest freestanding pinnacle? This phallus of granite rises some 400 feet above the ground at its upper edge and more than 1,000 feet on its downhill side. Naturally, it was to the upper side of the tower that the pioneers approached, for they wanted success, not an epic.

On the historic Sierra Club trip of Labor Day 1933—the first-ever climbers' visit to the Valley—Jules Eichorn, Dick Leonard, and Bestor Robinson had hiked up to the

Regular Route		Pitch				
		1	**2**	**3**	**4**	**5**
Free difficulty	≥5.10					
	5.9		●	●	●	
	5.8					●
	5.7					
	5.6					
	≤5.5	●				

southern base of the spire. Leonard's first impression: "After four hours of ineffectual climbing on the southwest face, and three hours more upon the southeast and east faces, we were turned away by the sheer difficulty of the climbing." It's no wonder they failed: their "pitons" on this reconnaissance were ten-inch-long nails!

On November 5, armed with pitons and carabiners obtained by mail from Sporthaus Schuster, a large sporting-goods store in Munich, the trio returned to the southern face and managed to climb two pitches before darkness forced a retreat. "By means of pitons as a direct aid," Leonard wrote, "we were able to overcome two holdless, vertical, ten-foot pitches..."

This attempt is historic, for it signified the first use of artificial aid in Yosemite—and one of the first times in the country. The technique of driving pitons into the rock in order to grab them, or to stand on them, or to attach slings to them—in other words, to use them to gain elevation—was common in the Alps. Robert Underhill, the trio's mentor, had trained in Europe and might have been expected to embrace this technique, but he was unyielding on the use of artificial aid: "Every pitch," he once wrote, "must be surmounted by one's own unaided abilities..." The pioneer Yosemite climbers respected Underhill, of course, but confronting firsthand the smoothness and sheerness of the Valley's cliffs, they realized they would not get far unless they used, occasionally at least, some form of "artificial" techniques. The trick, as they saw it, was to use as little direct aid as possible: the game was climbing, after all, not engineering. This adventurous attitude was to be emulated by most of the better climbers in the years to come.

After ordering more pitons from Sporthaus Schuster (they now possessed 55), the trio was set to go as soon as spring arrived. The Valley's first climbing spectators accompanied Eichorn, Leonard, and Robinson to the base of the Higher Spire on April 15, 1934, and present were two high-powered ones: Francis Farquhar, the president of the Sierra Club, and Bert Harwell, the park's chief naturalist, on hand to witness history. In a few hours the trio had reached their previous high point, a ledge at the base of a steep orange trough later known as the Rotten Chimney. Here, Eichorn and Leonard alternated pounding in the crude spikes, hanging on to them to inch upward. Where the crack ended, Leonard made a clever traverse to reach easier ground. Finally, as the Valley turned golden, the men nailed a last pitch to the spacious summit and planted an American flag—surely the only time this silly patriotic practice ever took place in Yosemite.

With the route known, the climb became popular almost immediately, though there were so few good climbers in the 1930s that only 12 ascents had been done by Pearl Harbor. Raffi Bedayn, that kind hearted soul who helped preserve Camp 4 in the 1970s, obviously loved the route: he did it four times between 1937 and 1941! Bill Hewlett, later to become famous as the co-founder of the Hewlett Packard organization, did the route in 1937—the eighth ascent. Though the first ascensionists had used lots of aid, this was naturally whittled down until by 1940 only ten feet of aid remained. This section, on the Bathtubs Pitch, was finally done free by Chuck Wilts and Spencer Austin in 1944.

– Steve Roper

Strategy

The best time to climb this route is between May and October. Most of the route is in the shade until about 1 p.m. so start early in the hot summer months and later during colder months. Most pitches are protected by a combination of gear and pervasive fixed pitons. Loose rock and tremendous exposure make this a climb best suited for confident and experienced 5.9 leaders. A single 60m rope is optimal and will allow you to rappel the route at convenient spots. The route can also be descended with a single 50m rope but this is not recommended.

The variations on the second pitch and last pitches offer steep and strenuous 5.9 crack climbing. Use these variations to add more crack climbing to the route or to pass slower parties.

Retreat

Retreat by rappelling the route with one 60m rope. The fourth belay is difficult to retreat from. If rappelling, be conscious of parties that may be climbing below.

More at SuperTopo.com

Get psyched for this route by visiting the route photo gallery for Higher Cathedral Spire. www.supertopo.com/rockclimbing/route.html?r=yohsregl

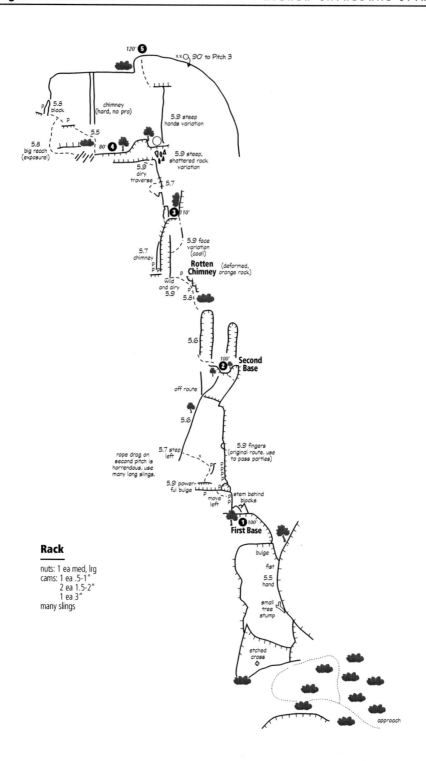

120' **5**

xx○ 90' to Pitch 3

p **5.8**
   block

chimney
(hard, no pro)

**5.9 steep
hands variation**

p

5.5

5.8
big reach
(exposure!)

80' **4**

**5.9 steep,
shattered rock
variation**

5.9
airy
traverse

5.7

3 110'

5.7
chimney

p

**5.9 face
variation
(cool!)**

**Rotten
Chimney** (deformed,
orange rock)

p

wild
and airy
5.9

p

5.8

5.6

100' **2** **Second
         Base**

off route

5.6

5.7 step
left

x

5.9 fingers
(original route, use
to pass parties)

rope drag on
second pitch is
horrendous, use
many long slings.

p

**5.9 power-
ful bulge**

move
left

stem behind
blocks

1 100'
First Base

bulge

fist

**5.5
hand**

small
tree
stump

etched
cross

approach

Rack

nuts: 1 ea med, lrg
cams: 1 ea .5-1"
      2 ea 1.5-2"
      1 ea 3"
many slings

Higher Cathedral Rock

Higher Cathedral Rock is one of the most ignored formations of the Valley, thanks to its modest position between its massive sibling, Middle Cathedral and the soaring phalluses of the Cathedral Spires. If HCR is hardly an earthshaking sight from the valley floor, the opposite is true once you stand beneath it. This is one steep and beautiful crag! And the bold buttress that shoots upward between the monolithic east face and the strangely unappealing north face is a true gem—colorful and mesmerizing.

– *Steve Roper*

Braille Book

Chris McNamara

Approach

If driving from Camp 4: take Northside Drive to El Capitan Meadow. Take a left at the triangle and drive east to just before you meet Southside Drive (the one way road). Park on the side of the road and walk 300 feet west on Southside drive to the pullout on the left (south). If driving into Yosemite Valley: on Southside Drive, park 300 feet before the turnoff to El Capitan Meadow at the paved pullout on the right.

From the middle of the pullout, locate a trail and walk 300 feet, passing a climbers' information sign, to the Valley Loop Trail. Turn left (east) and walk 300 feet until a climbers' trail is visible on the right. Follow this trail for 1-1.5 hours, at times scrambling over boulders, until a few hundred feet before the northeast face of Higher Cathedral Rock. Braille Book starts about 150 feet left of an enormous, ominous looking corner.

Descent

From the top of Braille Book, hike up and south for 150 feet, then cut left on a climbers' trail through brush. Follow the ridgetop down to the main notch between Higher Cathedral Rock and the valley wall. Follow the well-traveled climbers' trail as it switchbacks down through trees and brush onto talus. Hike down the talus until meeting the approach trail.

Braille Book

III 5.8★★★★

Time to climb route: **3-5 hours**

Approach time: **1-2 hours**

Descent time: **45 minutes-1.5 hours**

Sun exposure: **morning to afternoon**

Height of route: **700'**

An excellent climb in amazing surroundings and juggy face holds make the Braille Book a must-do. However, the cruxes all involve stemming on slick holds and/or flared chimneys and there is not always good protection. This is an old school 5.8 and will feel much harder if you do not have solid chimney skills. High points are the Cathedral Spires looming behind you, a surprise view of a giant chasm high on the route, and the unforgettable final pitch of huge 5.4 jugs on a steep, spectacular wall. While the hike is daunting for some, the trail is generally good, with limited boulder-hopping. The descent is neither treacherous nor long, and thus far fewer people are forced to bivy than one would expect for a long route high on a Valley wall.

History

Some routes aren't worth a long approach (the west face of North Dome springs to mind). Some routes definitely are. The approach to the Braille Book is not much fun: one must thrash up a steep, unpleasant forest and then ugly talus—1,800 vertical feet in all. But once this is out of the way, a delightful route awaits. When Jim Bridwell, Chris Fredericks, Brian Berry, and Joe Faint established this climb in June 1966, they knew they had a winner. Within weeks the quality line was repeated and word soon

spread. The origin of the name will be obvious to anyone who climbs the route: knobs abound and even a blind person could probably do the route. This is not to say the route is easy, as Bridwell protégé Jim Stanton realized one day. He fell high on the route, popped a few pitons, and plunged 160 feet. Incredibly, he escaped with only a knee injury.

- Steve Roper

Strategy

Unfortunately, the approach hike and hot summer temperatures don't keep the crowds down and many parties end up turning around due to the line. Getting an early start and moving fast up the 1800-foot slog is the solution, but others may have that idea. A great backup plan is to do the Regular Route of Higher Cathedral Spire— only a few hundred yards east of the start of Braille Book. A 50m rope is sufficient for Braille Book, since extending pitches with a 60m does not gain better belay points or allow linking pitches.

While jugs are everywhere on the first half of the route, the crux sections involve surprisingly burly moves, usually stemming off of slick holds, with some fist and offwidth moves. For the less experienced, the best possible practice for Braille Book is to work on flared stemming and flared chimneys. Some sections of chimney are protected only with micro-nuts.

Although high above the Valley floor, Braille Book is baked by summer sun until afternoon, and on hot days this is a route to avoid. Early season sees snow at the base and some wet sections. There are loose holds and blocks on the route, and as with any multi-pitch climb parties above always present some danger. Be aware that the bolts on this climb may not be safe.

Retreat

Retreat by rappelling from trees, your own gear, and/or bolts if you are high enough to gain the bolts on the new routes to the right. Two ropes are required unless you leave more gear.

Braille Book		1	2	3	4	5	6
Free difficulty	≥5.10						
	5.9						
	5.8	●	●	●	●		
	5.7					●	
	5.6						
	≤5.5						●

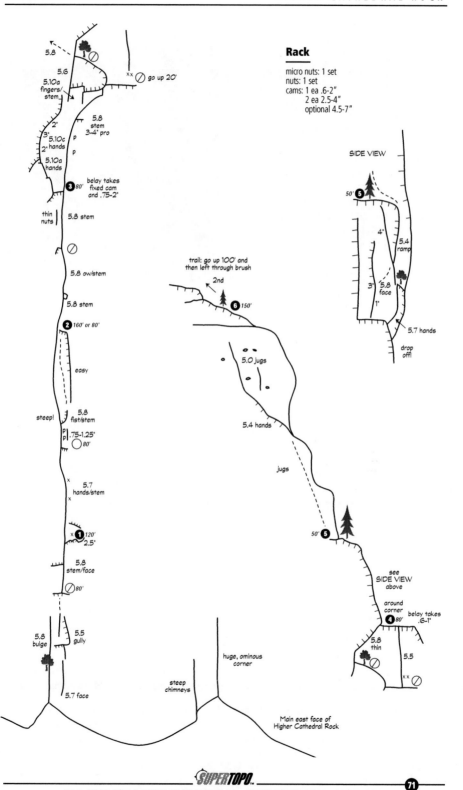

Rack

micro nuts: 1 set
nuts: 1 set
cams: 1 ea .6-2"
      2 ea 2.5-4"
      optional 4.5-7"

SIDE VIEW

5.8

5.6

5.10a
fingers/
stem

x x go up 20'

5.8
stem
3-4" pro

2"

3" 5.10c
2" hands

5.10a
hands

P
P

belay takes
fixed cam
and .75-2"

3 80'

thin
nuts

5.8 stem

5.8 ow/stem

5.8 stem

2 160' or 80'

easy

steep!

5.8
fist/stem

P
P .75-1.25"
    80'

x

5.7
hands/stem

x

x 1 120'
    2.5"

5.8
stem/face

80'

5.8
bulge

5.5
gully

5.7 face

huge, ominous
corner

steep
chimneys

trail: go up 100' and
then left through brush

2nd

6 150'

5.0 jugs

5.4 hands

jugs

50' 5

see
SIDE VIEW
above

around
corner

4 80'

belay takes
.6-1"

5.8
thin

5.5

x x

Main east face of
Higher Cathedral Rock

50' 5

4"

5.4
ramp

3' 5.8
    face

1"

5.7 hands

drop
off!

Middle Cathedral Rock

If Half Dome is forbidding, and El Cap smooth, then one must regard this rock as interesting, both to look at and to climb on. In certain lighting one can see thousands of the tiny ramps and flakes which makes climbing largely free and incredibly enjoyable. Much of the climbing consists of face climbing rather than cracks—this should come as a pleasant surprise to those who have thought the Valley is all nailing, 5.10 cracks and ghastly friction. Approaches to the routes are obvious—it is the descents which force people into occasional bivouacs.

— *Steve Roper,* Climber's Guide To Yosemite, *1971*

Chris McNamara

Approach

If driving from Camp 4: take Northside Drive to El Capitan Meadow. Take a left at the triangle and drive east to just before you meet Southside Drive (the one way road.) Park on the side of the road and walk 300 feet west on Southside drive to the pullout on the left (south). If driving into Yosemite Valley: on Southside Drive, park 300 feet before the turnoff to El Capitan Meadow on the paved pullout on the right.

From the middle of the pullout, locate a trail and walk 300 feet, passing a climbers' information sign, to the Valley Loop Trail.

From here, follow different trails depending on which route you are climbing:

Central Pillar of Frenzy
On the Valley Loop Trail, turn right (west) and walk 350 yards until you see the second carabiner post marking a climbers' trail. Walk up the hill to the base of the wall. Walk 50 feet right to the start of the route.

East Buttress
On the Valley Loop Trail, walk 300 feet right (west) until a climbers' trail is visible on the left marked by the first carabiner post. After 5 minutes the trail leads into a boulder-strewn gully. Follow the gully to a carabiner post in the middle of the boulders and another carabiner post to the

right marking a trail. After 150 feet you will reach a large platform with a great view of El Cap. The route starts here.

Descent

Central Pillar of Frenzy
Rappel on bolted anchors to the east of the climbing route (see topo.)

East Buttress
From the last belay, head right and up for 50 feet and then up and left on 3rd class. A trail becomes more distinct and contours left. After 250 feet look for a campfire ring/large cairns at a small clearing right before the first section of dense trees. Do not take the trail heading up and right. Instead, head down left through trees on a trail, which is not obvious at first. Follow the trail for 300 yards of easy but exposed 3rd class trail until it ends at the awesome chasm between Higher and Middle Cathedral Rocks. Scramble down this, with three single-rope rappels. Continue all the way down the gully, looking for the East Buttress approach trail (marked by carabiner posts) on the left at the point where trees close in almost at the bottom. Reverse the approach trail to the road.

East Buttress

IV 5.10c or 5.9 A0★★★★★

Time to climb route: **8-9 hours**

Approach time: **30-40 minutes**

Descent time: **1.5 hours**

Sun exposure: **morning to afternoon**

Height of route: **1100'**

Included in *Fifty Classic Climbs of North America*, the East Buttress clearly stands out as a Yosemite gem. Pitch after pitch of moderate Yosemite cracks are occasionally interrupted with short, well-protected crux sections. The view of El Capitan is astounding and only surpassed by the dreamy climbing moves. Solid protection and very few awkward wide sections make the East Buttress a great entry climb to long Yosemite 5.9s and 5.10s.

History

Middle Cathedral Rock rivals El Cap in an odd sort of way. It isn't as high or as monolithic or as majestic, but it certainly has more "character" than its cross-Valley neighbor. If El Cap is gray and forbidding, much of Middle is colorful and inviting. If El Cap defines Big Wall Climbing, then Middle stands for Medium Wall Climbing. What can be more intriguing than Yosemite's neglected orphan?

Warren Harding craved Middle long before he became fixated by the Big Stone. In May 1954 he had pioneered, with three others, the 2,000-foot north buttress of Middle, by far the longest roped climb yet done in North America. Three months later he shifted his eyes left to the shorter but much more compact east buttress. A few hundred feet above the ground, Harding,

Bob Swift, and John Whitmer twisted their way through an ant-infested tree (one of the little-known hazards of Valley climbing) and later arrived on a narrow platform below a crackless wall 40 feet high. This 65-degree slab was featureless, the biggest holds a mere quarter-inch wide. Any first ascensionist who wanted the east buttress would have to deal with this smooth wall, and no climber of the time (and very few today) could have done this unknown section free with zero protection. Artificial aid was needed and so out came the bolt kit. But down went the sun.

Bob Swift remembers the next events: "It was pitch dark when we heard voices below, in the forest. Some friends of ours were worried about us and had hiked up to check. They yelled up, 'How's the bivouac?' 'Bivouac? Hell, we're still climbing', was Warren's reply. The monotonous tink-tink of the hammer on the drill began again as work was started on the next bolt hole. Beside me on the belay ledge John rasped away furiously at sharpening a spare drill." Harding, later famous for his all-night drilling session on the first ascent of The Nose in 1958, had learned this nocturnal trick in 1954!

With the bolt ladder almost completed, they bivouacked and resumed climbing at dawn. The 50-foot section above the bolt ladder proved spectacular and thrilling. A long, serrated flake shot up the 70-degree wall, and the orange-colored granite was dotted liberally with knobs. It wasn't hard, yet it wasn't trifling either. One could rest on certain knobs and the protection was excellent. The exposure was sensational. But several pitches higher the trio ran out of steam and rappelled rather than face another bivouac.

East Buttress		Pitch 1	2	3	4	5	6	7	8	9	10	11
Free difficulty	≥5.10			•								
	5.9											
	5.8	•	•			•		•		•		
	5.7			•			•		•		•	•
	5.6	•										
	≤5.5											

The buttress now sported the longest continuous bolt ladder in the country—about nine. Bolts were not controversial back in 1954 and this ladder occasioned little comment at the time. In retrospect, however, this attempt can be seen as a radical Valley event. The old-timers had first sought out climbs with "inaccessible" summits like the Higher Spire and later routes that had natural lines, like the Column and Lower Brother. Harding was one of the first to see that hundreds of routes would open up if one simply placed a few bolt ladders to connect crack systems. (Much later, however, Harding's "excessive" use of bolts would cause a great rift in the climbing community.)

Little competition for routes existed in 1954 and Harding waited nine months before returning, knowing the route would remain virginal. Bob Swift and newcomer Jack Davis joined him on Memorial Day Weekend 1955, and thanks to the nine bolts, quickly reached the previous high point. After a bivouac near the top of the route, the trio finished the climb with alacrity and descended via the Kat Walk, the first ever to do so (William Kat, back in the 1920s, had wandered up this complex but easy route to the top of Middle). The Kat Walk later became the routine descent for many thousands of climbers.

Incredibly, this classic route was done only twice more during the 1950s. This obscurity was short-lived, however. A major variation—the one followed by most today—was put up in 1961 by Yvon Chouinard and Mort Hempel. Leaving the original route not far above the bolt ladder, this duo traversed up and right to a series of superb cracks that shot upward, meeting the original line three or four pitches higher. Hundreds of adventurers did the improved route in the early 1960s, but all used aid on the bolt ladder. Then, in 1965, the legendary Frank Sacherer climbed the bolt ladder free, a startling achievement for its time.

– *Steve Roper*

Strategy

Start early and bring a headlamp and warm jacket. Many people underestimate the length of the route and end up spending a night on the rock. Also, this is an exceptionally popular climb and you may have to wait behind slower climbers. Bring plenty of water.

The 5.10c crux on Pitch 5 is easy to avoid by pulling on the closely spaced bolts (no aiders needed). The climbing on the 50 Crowded Variation is excellent. This variation is easier than the bolt ladder and a great opportunity to pass bottlenecked parties.

After the crux pitch, there are two finishes to the climb. To the left, the original route heads up wide, strenuous and uncrowded terrain. To the right, Pitch 6 of the recommended route opens up with a spicy section of runout 5.6 and continues up stellar finger and hand cracks. A fall for the leader or follower will result in a pendulum.

Retreat

Two 50m or 60m ropes are required to retreat this route. The route can be rappelled from any pitch, but requires leaving gear at many belay points. Retreat after Pitch 5 is difficult because the route traverses to the right and left.

More at SuperTopo.com

In the spring of 2002 there was a large rock fall in the descent gully. Be sure to check the SuperTopo web site to see if the descent is safe. www.supertopo.com/rockclimbing/route.html?r=yomceast

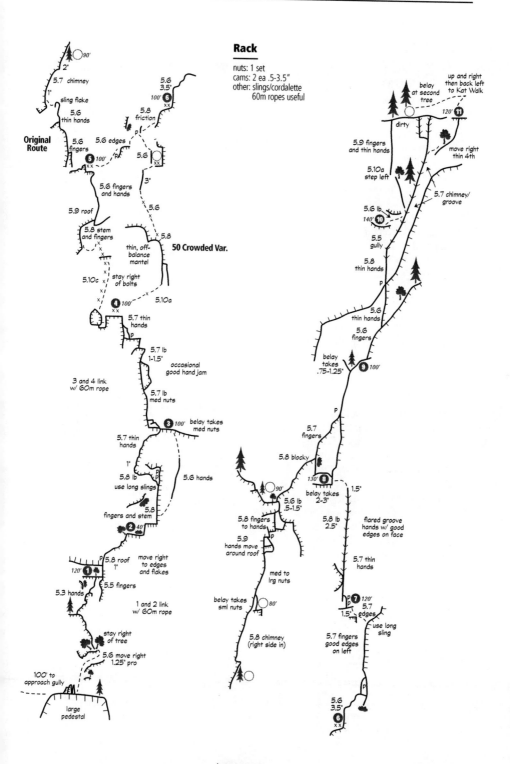

Rack

nuts: 1 set
cams: 2 ea .5-3.5"
other: slings/cordalette
60m ropes useful

Central Pillar of Frenzy

III 5.9★★★★★

Time to climb route: **4-6 hours**

Approach time: **15 minutes**

Descent time: **1-1.5 hours**

Sun exposure: **morning**

Height of route: **550'**

Rising from the heart of Middle Cathedral Rock, Central Pillar of Frenzy is one of the most popular 5.9 crack climbs in Yosemite. The route offers five pitches of excellent jamming with everything from fingers to chimney. The views of El Capitan (climbers are often visible) and the gentle emerald oxbows of the Merced River are spectacular.

History

Although Frenzy is a great name in itself, this route can be even better appreciated if one knows a little Alpine history. On the Italian side of Mont Blanc lie some huge and intimidating buttresses, one of which is called the Central Pillar of Frêney—for a short while the hardest climb in the Alps. It's admittedly a bit of a jump from Frêney to Frenzy, and from the Alps to the Valley, but that's the way the name came about, courtesy of Jim Bridwell, a fellow with a consuming passion for the history of climbing.

Middle Cathedral Rock's beautiful northeast face has many fine routes, but if you want to learn crack climbing, Frenzy is the place to go. Bridwell is responsible for this classic, and in 1973 he, Roger Breedlove, and Ed Barry did the first eight pitches. Two years later Bridwell returned with John Long and Billy Westbay to finish the route.

The route is famous now for its first five pitches, all of which involve 5.8 and 5.9 cracks. Liebacks, fist cracks, hand cracks, squeeze chimneys—you name it, you got it.

— Steve Roper

Strategy

Prepare to wait in line unless you begin extremely early in the morning. Be ready for uncomfortable belay stances and hanging belays. Do not leave food at the base as squirrels lurk in the talus waiting to scavenge through backpacks.

The first pitch is slippery and awkward, but protects well. The sustained wide section on Pitch 3 can be challenging, but a few extra 3.5-4" cams will enable those unaccustomed to wide cracks to protect it perfectly. Although most people rappel after Pitch 5, the route continues for another four pitches of less enjoyable 5.9 and hard 5.10. From Pitch 5, use the noted rappel route marked by Metolius hangers. Rappelling the climbing route is not recommended as it creates a danger for climbers below. In addition, ropes often get stuck on Pitch 3.

The route gets morning sun from late May through July, otherwise it is mostly shaded. In the summer, the route is less crowded and can have pleasant temperatures in the afternoon.

If the route is too crowded, but you want to get in a pitch of climbing, walk 250 feet west to Pee Pee Pillar. This 100-foot-long 5.10a climb is great for improving your finger crack, lieback, and stemming technique.

Retreat

Carry two 50m or 60m ropes for retreating from the route. Rappel from any point. From Pitch 5, follow the rap route shown on the topo.

More at SuperTopo.com

View mini trip reports and tons of climber beta for this route at:
www.supertopo.com/rockclimbing/
route.html?r=yomccent

Central Pillar of Frenzy	Pitch 1	2	3	4	5
Free difficulty ≥5.10					
5.9	●	●			●
5.8			●	●	
5.7					
5.6					
≤5.5					

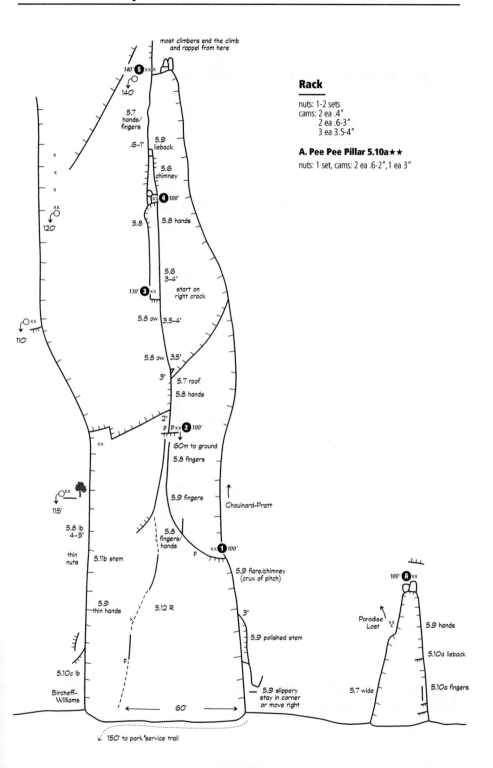

most climbers end the climb
and rappel from here

140' **5** xx xx

140'

5.7
hands/
fingers

.6-1"

5.9
lieback

5.6
chimney

4 100'

5.8   5.8 hands

5.6
3-4"

130' **3** xx   start on
right crack

5.8 ow 3.5-4"

5.8 ow 3.5"

3"   5.7 roof

5.8 hands

2" p P xx **2** 100'

60m to ground

5.8 fingers

5.9 fingers

Chouinard-Pratt

5.8
fingers/
hands

P   **1** 100'
xx

5.9 flare/chimney
(crux of pitch)

5.9
thin hands   5.12 R

3"

5.9 polished stem

5.9 slippery
stay in corner
or move right

60'

150' to park "service trail

120'

110'

115'
5.8 lb
4-5"

thin
nuts   5.11b stem

5.10c lb

Bircheff-
Williams

Rack

nuts: 1-2 sets
cams: 2 ea .4"
      2 ea .6-3"
      3 ea 3.5-4"

A. Pee Pee Pillar 5.10a★★

nuts: 1 set, cams: 2 ea .6-2", 1 ea 3"

100' **A** xx

Paradise
Lost   xx   5.9 hands

5.10a lieback

5.10a fingers

5.7 wide

MORE FROM SUPERTOPO

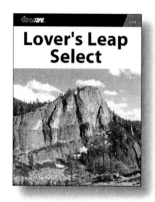

LAKE TAHOE'S CLIMBING GEM
LOVERS LEAP SELECT
List Price: $9.95 Available at www.supertopo.com

This guide includes virtually all the moderate classic climbs at Lover's Leap. Most of these climbs are well-protected, 2-4 pitches long, and ascend the incredible granite Lover's Leap is known for. Because these routes have so many face holds and good rests, they are the perfect introduction to granite trad climbing and outdoor climbing in general.

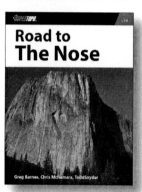

EVER WANTED TO CLIMB A BIG WALL?
ROAD TO THE NOSE
List Price: $14.95 Available at www.supertopo.com

Many climbers consider The Nose of El Capitan the crowning achievement of a climbing career. In the *Road to The Nose*, big wall master Chris McNamara takes you through 14 climbs of increasing difficulty to help you build skills, speed, endurance, and comfort with big wall climbing. This guide includes special tips and beta specific to The Nose as well as more general information on getting ready for your first big wall.

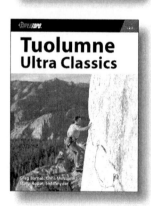

OUTSTANDING PEAKS AND DOMES IN THE HIGH SIERRA
TUOLUMNE ULTRA CLASSICS
List Price: $9.95 Available at www.supertopo.com

Spectacular rock and amazing views make Tuolumne Meadows a Sierra gem. With few tourists and cool temperatures this is an ideal summer destination for both face and crack climbing. This pack includes over 20 climbs in the 5.4 to 5.10 range including such classics as Cathedral Peak, Matthes Crest, West Crack, and Hobbit Book. There are enough routes in Tuolumne Ultra Classics for more than ten days of exceptional climbing.

Also Available from SuperTopo.com

Road to Astroman - A collection of dream climbs for aspirant 5.10 and 5.11 climbers.
Desert Towers Select - A collection of Utah's classic moderate towers.
High Sierra Select - Finally, detailed and accurate topos of California's High Sierra.
Yosemite Big Walls - The ultimate guide for big wall climbing in Yosemite Valley.

About the Authors

Greg Barnes

Greg has been climbing since '94, and he can tell you every move on every route he's done, draw a topo from memory, give you his opinion on the rating of any pitch, repeat anything written in any guidebook about it, and tell you about the weather that day. He is Director of the American Safe Climbing Association. From 1998 to June 2002, Greg replaced 121 bolts in Yosemite Valley by hand drilling, which takes 20-30 minutes of pounding per bolt. From Central Pillar of Frenzy to Stoner's Highway to Astroman to the Nose, Greg has worked hard to make climbing safer for all of us. Please support him and the other volunteers of the ASCA by visiting www.safeclimbing.org and donating!

Greg lives in Bishop, Yosemite, Tuolumne, Joshua Tree, and Red Rocks and develops SuperTopos for these areas.

Chris McNamara

Climbing Magazine once computed that three percent of Chris McNamara's life on earth has been spent on the face of El Capitan—an accomplishment that has left friends and family pondering Chris' sanity. He's climbed El Capitan over 50 times and holds nine big wall speed climbing records. In 1998 Chris did the first Girdle Traverse of El Capitan, an epic 75-pitch route that begs the question, "Why?" Outside Magazine has called Chris one of "the world's finest aid climbers." He's the winner of the 1999 Bates Award from the American Alpine Club and founder of the American Safe Climbing Association, a nonprofit group that has replaced over 3,000 dangerous anchor bolts. He also serves on the board of directors of the Access Fund.

Steve Roper

Roper was never much of a fan of topos until now. "Routes were vague back in the old days," he says, "and by using vague words we guidebook writers could ensure that climbers would get just as lost as we did." Later, when topos first appeared, he saw their usefulness but was disgusted by their crude appearance. And a wordless description meant that the history of the route was also lost, perhaps forever. In Roper's many books about climbing and backpacking, he stresses history, feeling it's an integral part of the overall experience. "Think of doing the Nose without knowing the name Warren Harding!" The skeptic Roper now is at peace with SuperTopos, feeling that a few hundred well-chosen words placed next to a beautifully drawn topo is the best of all worlds.

Todd Snyder

Todd's impressive credentials include Yosemite Search and Rescue, guiding for Yosemite Mountaineering School and structural engineering work on top-secret supersonic aircraft somewhere in the California desert. He has been climbing for over 15 years and has climbed and/or guided climbers on nearly every great climb in Yosemite Valley. In 1998 he was featured in the climbing instructional video, "Introduction to Aid Climbing." He is currently Operations Manager for Corey Rich's photo business, Coreography. You can see some of Todd's outstanding work by downloading our free SuperTopo of Half Dome's classic Snake Dike.